Lost and Found in Mexico

Kirk House Publishers

Lost and Found in Mexico

A Widow's Road to Recovery

CANDY WOLFF

Lost and Found in Mexico: A Widow's Road to Recovery
© Copyright 2024 by Candy Wolff

First Printing: May 2024
First Edition

Paperback ISBN: 978-1-959681-60-1
eBook ISBN: 978-1-959681-61-8
Hardcover ISBN: 978-1-959681-62-5
LCCN: 2024908216

Interior and cover design by Ann Aubitz
Cover art by Rachel Thompson.
Author headshot by Anne Lang

Published by Kirk House Publishers
1250 E 115th Street
Burnsville, MN 55337
kirkhousepublishers.com
612-781-2815

Dedication

With heartfelt love and gratitude, I give praise to God. Your presence in my life brings me true joy.

To my wonderful sons, Zach, Eli, and Noah: This book and Ross's enduring legacy are dedicated to you. Since Ross's passing, you have been my pillars of strength. Though my role as your mother was to care for you, you have cared for me this past year. I'm deeply thankful for my faith in Jesus and for having such remarkable sons. Navigating life without Ross has been challenging, but together, we continue this journey. We miss his wisdom and guidance every day.

To my dear family and friends who have supported me through the last 14 months, from the moment I decided to write this book, you have been my cheerleaders. Your encouragement helped me overcome many obstacles, and you were always just a phone call away when I needed a listening ear or words of motivation. Your unwavering support and love have propelled me forward to where I am today.

To my love, Ross: I'm at peace knowing you have found rest in heaven and are free from pain. This book reflects the journey you helped guide me on, from our dating days to our marriage and through your passing. You always encouraged me to reach my full potential and inspired me to be the best version of myself. Because of your influence, I have grown stronger, more courageous, confident, and more independent each day. Until we meet again, you will forever hold a cherished place in my heart and in the hearts of our sons.

Acknowledgements

Ahtziri, you held my hand the moment I lost Ross, made sure that I ate when I didn't want to, and were there for hugs, constantly reassuring me it would be okay. You told me to go talk to Ross and God on the beach daily! You even suggested I take him to the beach that last night to talk to him! I'm sure everyone walking by was wondering what this crazy lady was doing, crying and talking to a box! What they didn't know was my husband's ashes were in that box. My family and I love you, and they take comfort in knowing that I had you, my angel, and the amazing bellmen—Juan, Eliel, Dago, Armando, Efrain—by my side during the three days following Ross's death!

Thank you to my parents, my mother-in-law, and all my family. You saved me from despair, and I will never forget that as long as I live.

Rich, thank you for being a rock for me and for my in-laws. You called and texted multiple times a day, not only while I was in Mexico but for months after. You are Ross's best friend and made sure I knew I wasn't alone. You reached out to many of the White Bear friends I didn't know to let them know the horrible news. The fact that you two were friends since second grade is astonishing, but the fact that you make sure the boys and I are good is something Ross is smiling down on, saying, "That's why he was my best friend."

To Zach, Eli, and Noah, my love for you is so much greater than you will ever know. Thank you for loving me thorough out this last year as it has been difficult on all of us. You are my whole world.

Table of Contents

Foreword

You know, there are a lot of people who talk about the importance of faith. They say that they believe in a higher power, or they believe in some cosmic being, or they believe the universe is just going to provide for them if they speak it into existence. Other people have a whole different kind of faith. A kind of faith that is built on the hope that this is not the end. That there is another experience waiting for you at the end of this journey here on earth.

And that faith can be life-changing! But you never really know if that's the kind of faith you have until it's been tested. Until there's a morning that's supposed to start like any other morning only to leave you utterly exhausted. To leave you searching for answers, screaming at the sky, and asking God why! How could you…or this doesn't make any sense!

Have you ever had one of those moments? Have you ever asked that question? No…Yes…Maybe you're asking it right now! Maybe it's the reason you picked up this book. Let me just tell you, it is in those moments that the faith you say you have is tested. It is those moments you reveal to yourself how strong your beliefs, your convictions are.

A couple of years ago I had the privilege of getting to know an incredible couple at this new church that I just took over. Don't run because you just found out that I work at a church, I'm not the one who wrote this book, what I do doesn't matter but who I know…that's what is going to benefit you on whatever journey you find yourself on as you read this book.

In 2019 I took over a small church as a campus pastor. That was right before COVID ended up shutting down that very small very struggling church, and I had no idea what was going to happen next. But through that process, I made a great friend two great friends.

I got to know Ross and Candy well over the summer of 2020. We had a variety of projects around the church and Ross always had a willingness to jump in and help me with plumbing, lighting, or general repairs.

Side note: If you want to know a great way to connect with another dude, do projects with them. Shoulder-to-shoulder time breaks through barriers with some guys a lot faster than face-to-face time. Through that time, I got to hear from Ross about his wife, a wife that he adored, and would do anything on the planet for.

I learned about his faith, his questions, his past, his present, his joys, his pains, and how Candy was there with him in and through all of it. Candy's commitment to Ross is inspiring. There are a ton of relationships built on a contract. Essentially, as long as each person lives up to whatever prearranged expectations they will stay together. However, there always seems to be a limit or a shelf-life once things start to get difficult.

When job loss hits, or medical issues arise, or fill in the blank. I think you get what I am saying. They are all in as long as things are all good. Candy's resolve to walk with Ross, hand-on-hand, side-by-side, and even with him slung over her shoulder to help him walk (not just a good word picture but an actual occurrence when Ross's hips were failing him at a young age).

Ross was a man who was determined to fight through it—no matter what IT was—to be the best he could for his bride. And Candy is a woman who showed her faithfulness to her husband and was determined to love him through it—no matter what IT was. A relationship built on love and forged in faith.

Well, Candy had no idea just how hot the forging fire was about to get, not just for her commitment to Ross but to her God. I know you've been there, or perhaps you are there right now. Fists clinched to the air, shouting to the heavens, or in silent despair and desperation. If that's you,

I know how hard that place is, and stories of faith in people just like you can provide the example of hope you need. Where you are is not the place it has to end. The pain, the hurt, the doubts don't have to be the end of the story. Candy is living proof—your faith can sustain the refining fire of pain, hurt, fear, doubt, and confusion.

Maybe, you're not there yet. Maybe you're like, "Pastor Chad, my life is pretty good, I don't have a context for that." Let me just say this, I am so glad that is true for you. WHEN the hard things happen you will be able to draw from this story of an incredibly resilient woman who experienced miracle after miracle of God proving He is worth believing in. He is worth trusting when the fire gets too hot to stand on your own…there is another in the fire who will sustain you. He will show up in ways you never imagined, just like He did for Candy. Don't believe me? Proof lives in the following pages.

~Pastor Chad Melton

Chapter 1

From Promise to Peril

*You know how many months we will live, and
we are not given a minute longer.*
~Job 14:15

My husband's cheek was purple like a moonless sky, and his body thick with the weight of death. I knew he was gone. Still, I couldn't stop screaming. Before reason had a chance to set in, I went to a dark place in my mind, pronouncing him dead of an accidental overdose.

Those were the worst seconds of my life. I wish I could say that everything got better, but it didn't. All I know now is the phone shouldn't ring that early, and Mexico should be a place of rebirth—not the thing that steals your joy.

It feels like yesterday and a million years ago, but I can still hear that phone buzzing in my ear. I'm asleep in the hotel with my husband, Ross, and it's 7:11 a.m., Friday,

January 27th, 2023. I reach over to pick it up and hear my mechanic telling me my car is ready. I say, "Great, let me call my son in Minnesota to arrange for pickup." And I end the call.

I glance over and notice Ross isn't moving. I get up and walk around the bed because his head is kind of buried to the side, and the sheet is up. I grab his feet; they're cold. I climb onto the bed and sit there, feeling his entire body, searching for warmth.

I know he's not alive. I try to roll him over; rigor mortis has set in. Finally, I manage to turn him enough to see the side of his cheek, where it's purple. I start screaming, pounding on him, begging him to wake up. I keep screaming at God to make him wake up.

Then I'm sitting there, asking, "God, what do we do? What do I do?" I pick up the hotel phone and dial zero. Someone answers, and all I can say is, "My husband's dead. My husband's dead."

The voice on the other end remains calm, "Are you sure? We're sending a doctor."

I reply, "He's purple. I think he overdosed."

"Can you unlock your door, please? Go unlock your door," the voice instructs.

I go and unlock the door, leaving it open.

I try to walk back but drop to my knees, screaming and crying. The voice on the other end of the phone reassures me, "Just breathe. I'm here, and I'm going to stay with you until someone arrives."

Within minutes, two security guards and a doctor arrive. They roll Ross over, but it's clear he's gone. The doctor puts an oximeter on his finger, and I almost laugh. All I can think is "Are you kidding me?" He is putting an oximeter on a cold purple finger, and I'm saying to myself, "Oh, my God. Where am I?"

With their exit, the room shrinks, and it's just Ross and me. I'm holding him in my arms as I drift back to that beautiful season when our paths first crossed.

It's the year 2006, and I'm about to divorce my first husband. His struggles with gambling and drinking have taken a toll on our family, which includes three young sons, Zach, Eli, and Noah.

My brother and sister-in-law had convinced us to move to Arizona for a fresh start on our marriage. We had put our house in Montana on the market, which took three long months to sell. During this time, I was left alone with the kids, handling the house preparations and the impending move.

Finally, in late August, he arrives in Montana to move us back with him to Arizona. It's Labor Day weekend, but his distant demeanor signals the end of our relationship. By early October, I decide it's time for a divorce. I need stability for my children, so I secure a job at Jackson Trailers in Glendale, Arizona, where I can work and provide for my family.

During my first few weeks at work, Ross, a charming and handsome stranger, walks through the door. Out of all the people I've seen, he stands out. Ross has recently moved from Minnesota, also going through a divorce, and is opening a West Coast office. He's there to exchange a snowmobile trailer for an enclosed one suitable for four-wheelers.

We strike up a conversation, and Ross's first words to me are, "Where did you come from?" I reply, "Montana." He says, "I am from Minnesota." Our shared love for hockey and mutual interests sparks a connection. I can't help but notice his striking green suit. He looks so handsome. I don't know it yet, but that suit will become a favorite of mine. Every time he wears it, in our future together, I will remember this moment.

As we talk, Ross learns I'm in the process of divorcing, marked by the absence of my wedding ring. The chemistry is undeniable, and we embark on a journey that will change our lives forever.

I'm 33, and Ross is 38. Ross doesn't have any kids of his own, but there's something about him that just feels right. Whenever I see him, I get those butterflies in my stomach.

One day, Ross returns to the store where I work, dressed sharply in his suit. It's a week after his birthday. We start talking, and I suggest we celebrate with his best friend Rich, who moved with him to Arizona and my good friend Crystale who moved with my family from Montana. That's when we exchange phone numbers and begin texting.

I'm upfront with him, telling him I have three kids, and surprisingly, it doesn't faze him. We start going on dates when my kids are with their dad. Ross is different from anyone I've known. He's a gentleman, kind, and he makes me feel special.

One evening, we have dinner at a quaint little restaurant, and Ross orders me wine. It's then that he tells me he's a recovering alcoholic. I admire his strength and honesty. Our connection grows stronger, and I continue to get those butterflies.

Eventually, Ross meets my kids, and they quickly take to him. It's clear that Ross cares deeply for my children. One day, Noah is jumping on the bed in his room while I'm making everyone dinner. Suddenly, a shrill cry pierces the air, and Ross's panicked voice joins in, "Oh, shit, he broke the dresser." But it's not just the dresser; Noah has managed to split his head wide open.

I rush in and see Ross is distressed, calling out, "Noah, Noah!" It seems Noah's playful jump ended in an unexpected catastrophe. The dresser knobs gave way, leaving a trail of blood in their wake. My immediate focus is on keeping Noah alert, reassuring Ross that he'll be okay.

In the midst of the chaos, I grab a washcloth and start cleaning up the mess, determined to keep Noah awake and comforted. Ross, overwhelmed by guilt and worry, exclaims, "Oh my God, I almost killed your kid." It's moments like these that remind me just how deeply he cares for these children, which also keeps those familiar butterflies fluttering within me.

Our courtship is relatively short, but it's filled with adventures. In 2008, Ross asks us to move in with him. He treats my kids as if they're his own, taking them four-wheeling, hiking, and on trips. Ross is a support system for me, even though the boys aren't his biological children. He supports me in every way possible.

Not long after we move in together, Ross receives a transfer offer that relocates us to Colorado, and he asks us to join him in Denver. Before we have a chance to fall completely in love with the mountains there, Ross tells us to pack our bags again, this time for the snowy plains of Minnesota. Just before our final move as a family, Ross proposes and we get married, not with a grand ceremony, but by a judge in a casual setting.

We marry in June of 2009 and move to Minnesota in July of 2009. Ross remains a pillar of support for my children, coaching their sports teams and always trying to connect with them. He provides for their every need and more. We face challenges, but Ross's care and love for my kids never waver. Even in times of financial strain, he never hesitates to give them what they want.

Now, looking back, I laugh at the unexpected turns our relationship took. Ross and I, both initially hesitant about marriage, find ourselves bound together in love, and my kids gain a remarkable father figure. We compromise constantly and find ways to bring each other joy, even agreeing to something as absurd as a beachfront log cabin for our future retirement home. With Ross having always dreamt of living in a log home and me insisting on a beach locale, we settle on a mix of both! Life isn't always easy, but it's filled with love, adventure, and support.

Zach, my oldest, ends up moving out in the summer going into his sophomore year of high school after a dispute over an Xbox cord. Ross had removed it to encourage Zach to get his grades up, but Zach wasn't swayed. I decide to let Zach go live with his dad in Montana. It's a tough choice to let him go, but I know that's what he wanted, so he returned to Montana, living with his dad and grandparents, and has a good life there.

Ross, my rock, supports my decision to let Zach go, and shoulders the burden of my grief. Time passes, and Zach realizes the value of the family we've created. He apologizes to me and builds a closer bond with Ross. Eli, who was just three and a half when he met Ross, always sees him as a father figure.

As for Noah, Ross has been there from day one, and Noah considers him his dad. Our journey has its ups and downs, but the love and support Ross gives our kids makes all the difference.

Over the years, Ross never wavers. When Eli graduates, Ross buys him a generous gift—a $10,000 truck. At first, I think it's extravagant, but it's more a reflection of Ross's desire for the truck. Two weeks later, Zach gets married, and we help with a portion of the wedding expenses and gift him $2,000. We're in a comfortable financial position at the time, traveling often, and ensuring our kids have everything they need.

Our love story was like no other, and every memory of our time together is etched into my heart. It's a tale of love, laughter, and unwavering support. There's not much I can say about my life with Ross that hasn't been said by a woman in love before. It was amazing. We were happy. That's what truly set us apart. We clung to the good times and wrestled through the dark times. But we did it all together. Or so I thought.

In 2018 our world takes a sudden turn. Ross is called into work on June 26th and unexpectedly laid off, marking a significant change in his life and ours. Just three months later, Ross's dad passes away. Having always been a private person, Ross wants to maintain appearances, but the fact is, losing his dad and his dream job after 20 years due to corporate reshuffling is crushing. The company is sold to new owners who scrutinize the numbers, looking to boost profits, and they ax the top earners, including Ross. Despite the significant revenue that Ross brings in, he's out. Right away, he seeks counseling and spends time with our pastors. As job opportunities arise, he gets excited, pursuing every lead, only to find their salaries meager and roles entry to mid-level.

In his final years, Ross works for a couple of companies, but it's nothing like in his heyday. To make matters worse, his health begins to deteriorate. By September of 2022, just four months before he dies, Ross undergoes a total hip and knee replacement. Regrettably, he never commits to post-surgery exercises, suffering constant pain.

I am the only one who knows the extent of his pain, and every now and then he lets on that we're struggling financially as well. I know that he's tapping into our 401k, but I'm uncertain about the extent since I've been consistently working.

Miraculously, he is able to maintain his sobriety and is planning to celebrate 29 years without a drink on March 13, 2023. However, deprived of a steady income, Ross feels powerless. Desperation sets in, and our dreams of travel and a beachfront log cabin remain distant. Still, on the edge of 50, I tell Ross I want to go to Cabo to celebrate my birthday.

Every time Ross and I visit Mexico, it's like stepping into a fairytale. Our go-to destination is our friend Vass's stunning retreat. It is nestled within a secure, gated community affectionately dubbed the "Beverly Hills of Cabo." From the moment we are whisked away from the airport, the enchantment of the place washes over us.

Securing a coveted week at Vass's house feels like a stroke of serendipity for us. However, coordinating my 50th birthday getaway proves a delicate task. Zach and his wife Shelbie already have their sights on an upcoming cruise, Eli has just started a promising new job, and Noah is busy.

As for Vass's house, it is already booked, so we have to, for the first time in our lives, make other plans.

One evening after work, Ross excitedly exclaims, 'We can go to Cabo for $89!' I'm taken aback and inquire, 'How?' He replies, "With our Delta points and e-credits we can make it happen, just $89, you and me, for a week." I enthusiastically respond, "Book it!"

This is when I realize that our financial situation might be dire. Our vacations used to cost thousands of dollars, but now every expense seems significant. Additionally, Ross's health and stress due to surgeries play a role. In the past year, we've spent little time together because he's often in bed, and I'm either working or with the kids.

We grow apart, and I continuously urge him to seek more help for his depression. I suspect that he hasn't revealed the full extent of his struggles. This trip to Cabo couldn't come at a better time. Spending a week together on the beach, reconnecting, and having fun is just what we need.

Every night leading up to the trip, we discuss our favorite places to eat and explore the resort's offerings. Cabo, our most cherished destination, our heaven on earth is finally in reach.

And I suppose, if a volcano of emotion and financial turmoil is going to erupt, it should be beside the Pacific Ocean.

Chapter 2

Paradise Turned Nightmare

To everything there is a season, and a time for every matter or purpose under heaven.
~Ecclesiastes 3:1

Villa del Palmar Beach Resort is a luxurious getaway nestled along the stunning Baja California Peninsula in Cabo San Lucas. It's the perfect blend of natural beauty and modern amenities. Ideally located on a pristine stretch of Medano Beach, the resort is framed by iconic rock formations and the azure waters of the Sea of Cortez.

Rooms feature private balconies overlooking the ocean. There's a multi-level pool complete with cascading waterfalls, swim-up bars, and hot tubs, all surrounded by lush gardens and towering palm trees.

The staff is there to pamper and cater to your every need. It's a place where guests can truly unwind, make memories, and savor the beauty of Mexico. For couples,

Villa del Palmar is about reconnecting, growing closer, and renewing vows. For me and Ross, it was about saying goodbye.

I'm in the room, alone with Ross. I look at his cross, the one I bought him. I sense the presence of God, compelling me to remove it from him. My thoughts keep repeating in my head, take his cross off, take his cross off. I have to struggle with his stiff body, but eventually I get it off and slip it in my pajama pocket.

Just then, a woman rushes in from guest services. I don't know it then, but she's an angel sent by God. Her name tag reads Ahtziri, and she immediately offers her support. She asks, "Hi Candy! I am so sorry for your loss. I am here to help you, and you can trust me. Where's your husband's phone? We have to find it. Where is it?"

My mind is in disarray, and I have no idea where anything is scattered around the room.

She continues, "Where's your phone?" I respond, "It's right here in my pocket." Right then, the first set of police officers arrives just as she grabs Ross's phone from the nightstand. I watch her discreetly pocket it. She never says so, but it's later clear to me that if she hadn't found his phone, I might never have seen it again.

"We must move you to another room. The police have to seal off this one," she says.

The rest of the day is a blur. The police officers come in to inspect everything. They instruct me, just as Ahtziri did, to leave, even though I'm still in my pajamas. I go to grab my purse, and the police say, "Put it down. You can't take anything with you, this is a crime scene." Ahtziri ushers me downstairs to another room.

The embassy calls to offer their condolences. I don't recall the exact words, but they assure me that someone from the only funeral home in Cabo will be here to assist me shorty. They emphasize that if I need anything, I should contact them, and they ask for my email address. However, in my grief, I accidentally give them the wrong email because my dad somehow gets involved, and they end up emailing him instead.

Time stands still. All I do is pace the floor and constantly check my phone for messages from home. After what seems like hours, the funeral service coordinator, Yadira, arrives and makes me recount the events of the day. I tell her how I woke up and he was cold. But my mind is overwhelmed by thoughts of the pain pills Ross had been taking, and I fear the presence of fentanyl.

I have been texting friends and family all morning to share my concerns. Over and over, I find myself writing the words, "I believe he overdosed." Regrettably, that thought dominates my mind, and it's the message I convey to everyone I talk to, except the police, during that agonizing morning.

One vivid memory stands out—my call to Ross's mother, Sandie. Her voice, filled with disbelief, echoes through the phone, "How could he overdose? He's been sober. How could he?"

And I said, "He was in so much pain." We just sat and cried because we both knew how much pain he had been in.

I knew Ross was taking pills because I went with him just to keep an eye on what was going to be bought. The first pharmacist we talked to sold him opioids, no problem, but the second pharmacist said he could only sell him muscle relaxers unless he had a prescription. So, we walk across the street to a third pharmacist, and they sell him more opioids.

Throughout the trip, I keep telling him he needs to be careful. I don't know how much he is taking, but I am worried about him. That day, he looks at me and says, "You have no idea how much pain I'm in. If I can take a couple of pills that will get me through the day and I don't have to think about it, I'm going to do it. Otherwise, I will pack my stuff and go home. And you can stay here, but you're not going to tell me what to do." I say, "You're a grown man, and I can't tell you what to do."

Yadira pulls me back from my thoughts to the present nightmare and asks, "What would you like to do? Cremation? Or do you want us to send his body back?" I immediately reply, "I'm not leaving here without him. I came with him, and he's going home with me." We agree on cremation, but she tells me the autopsy must be completed first.

The phone rings. Ahtziri answers, speaking in Spanish, I sense it's a call from the police. She pauses to confirm and tells me they have finished their investigation. She says the coroner is here to take Ross and that the police are asking if I want to see him first. Thinking this might be the last time I ever see my husband, I agree.

As I stand to my feet, a fog washes over me, pulling me back to the last words I spoke to Ross, just 14 hours ago.

There's this place we always dine at in Cabo. I tell Ross I really want to go there. He's not himself, but I try to coerce him anyway. Depression seems to have gotten the best of him, and I know his knee is giving him grief, especially after that walk on the beach.

I figure he is tired and needs some extra rest and maybe I'll go eat—and maybe find my new friends we met at the resort, two wonderful couples, one from Mendota Heights and one from Canada. Throughout the week, I spend time with them while Ross is dozing off, occasionally waking up, but overall, he is constantly fatigued and not himself.

By Thursday night, I am overcome with loneliness. I walk down to the beach and find a chair to lounge in. I call my oldest son, Zach, and tell him something feels terribly wrong. Tears stream down my face as I share my concerns. I tell him that Ross has bought pain pills during our trip, but I didn't know how many he's taken. I lament my gut feeling that he might overdose. "He's been sleeping so much, Zach," I say. "It seems all he wants to do is sleep, and it's worrying me."

After our call, I head back to the room. It's around 9 o'clock, and Ross is lying in bed with the TV on, still sleeping. I think, "Well, I guess I'll get ready for bed. We're leaving in a couple of days." I take a shower and brush my teeth. It is 10ish; he still has the lights on and is snoring quite loudly. I have restless legs, so I decide to sleep on the pull-out bed with a headband to block out the noise.

I reach over to turn off the lights. Ross rolls over and looks at me, asking, "What are you doing?" I reply, somewhat upset, "Well, I guess I'm going to bed because you're asleep, and I don't have much else to do." He simply says, "Fine," rolls over, and I turn off the light. Little do I know that the next morning, I will find that he's passed away in the night.

No, "I love yous." No, "See you in the morning." Just a quiet, unassuming "Fine!" I carry the weight of that memory with me as I stagger through the halls of this once-glorious hotel.

When I get to the room, three bellmen are there. One I connect with immediately. His name is Eliel, which is so similar to my son Eli's name; I can't help but be drawn to him. There's yellow tape across the door, and the coroner is in the hallway with a cart ready to whisk my love away. I reach for Eliel's arm to keep myself from falling. He knocks on the door, and an officer swings it wide, revealing a scene straight out of a horror movie.

I have to walk around the kitchenette, past the officer, before I can see that they've rolled Ross completely over. He looks ghastly and nothing like himself. I fall to my knees. The bellmen grab me and carry me over to him. I just sit with him as they tell me to take my time. I hug him and tell him how much I love him. I say, "I don't understand how this happened, but I know you're in a better place." I keep telling him that. I say, "I know you're not hurting anymore. You're with God. He took you from me for a reason. I don't know why, but I know there is a reason. I love you so much!"

I was with him for ten minutes. Then the coroner says we have to take him.

The room is in disarray. It looks like a police raid, with drawers pulled out and all our stuff on the floor in a big pile. Eliel brings in a cart and begins loading the mess the police have made.

I'm distraught and unable to focus. As we load the cart, I see all the food we'd bought for our trip. All I can think of is telling everyone to take the food. I fear it will go to waste and become obsessed with passing every morsel off to these wonderful people who have become my lifeline. I urge everyone in the room to take the food home to their families. I keep insisting and they hesitate. Perhaps out of fear of upsetting me more, they barely speak. I am firm, saying, "Take it. I don't want it. I won't eat it. You need it more than I do. If you don't divide it, I'll do it right now." I am completely out of sorts, my mind in a haze, unable to focus on anything. They can see this and agree to take the food.

Ahtziri and the bellmen escort me to a different location within the building, on the first floor. I vividly remember being led into a room. Ahtziri explains that we need to go through my belongings. Together, we compile a list of missing items. We discover that my husband's wallet, as well as mine, are empty. Ross's cigars are missing, two pairs of Oakley sunglasses, clothing—even contact lenses, of all things—are gone. It seems the police have stolen these items, along with two high-quality phone charging sets.

Ahtziri asks me if I want to file a report, and I say, "File a report to who? The police?" Still, we document everything on the list so that if the housekeepers come across these items, it will be accounted for.

Day turns into night, and nothing matters except that time keeps marching on. It's Saturday now, and I have no idea what might happen next. Ahtziri informs me that Yadira needs me to attend an interview. She has no information about where it will take place or who I'll be speaking with, only that a car will arrive soon to pick me up. Around 8 a.m., I step into a dark car and see Yadira at the wheel. She and I begin the uncertain journey. As we drive, I remain calm on the surface, but inside, I'm filled with dread.

I'm plagued by thoughts of this interview. In my mind, perhaps it's with the coroner, the one who has Ross's body. Maybe we're going to her office at the funeral home to meet with more people I've never met. All I know is nothing can prepare me for what I'm about to endure.

We drive through unfamiliar streets, and she points out various landmarks. My anxiety is tempered by an odd sense of calm. We pass by locations like where Ross will be cremated and what appears to be her office, yet we continue driving. The uncertainty gnaws at me, and I instinctively reach for my phone, sending a message to my brother-in-law, Reed. It reads, "FYI, I'm in the car with the lady from the funeral home, I don't know where we are going. I just need you to know who I am with. Please be by your phone. I don't know what's going on." The impending destination remains a mystery.

Finally, I gather the courage to inquire about the interview's location. She casually informs me that it's at the police station, where I'll face their interrogation. Panic surges within me, and I feel nauseous.

My fingers fly across my phone as I send a message to Reed: "I don't know if I'm coming home. I have to go talk to the police!"

Panic threatens to overwhelm me, but Reed's reply brings me back to sanity. His message says, "Just breathe."

Leaving the car, I nearly collapse because I don't know if I'll ever emerge from that place. Inside, my heart rate monitor is going haywire, my watch indicating abnormally high readings—not surprising given the circumstances. We enter a decrepit building: an old police station, with dilapidated furniture. Communication is challenging; no one speaks English or attempts to.

They guide me into a room with three desks, two chairs, a large man, an even bigger man, and a girl typing, all wearing stern expressions. I muster a greeting, saying, "Hi." The girl tells me to sit down. The seating is arranged in such a way that the desk is in between, and I lean forward to catch a glimpse of the file that reads "Ross Lindsay Walhof" and another that says, "Candice Mae Wolff." I lean back, still clutching my phone, which they haven't confiscated. I text, "They have a file on me." My brother-in-law texts back, reassuring me, "Candy, just breathe. Keep breathing." He mentions having an attorney on speed dial, ready to assist me when needed and tells me to simply text "YES" and he'll make the call.

I am struggling to catch my breath, overwhelmed. Meanwhile, they are conversing, speaking in a language I can't comprehend, except for the phrase "Moi Frio," which I keep repeating to convey that he felt cold.

We must have been here for at least four hours, and I haven't spoken much. They start asking about any markings on him. I struggle to think clearly, saying, "He has a tattoo on his leg, near the ankle." Yadira is translating, but I struggle to find the right words. Eventually, I manage to convey that it's a happy smiley face, which they seem unable to comprehend. I resort to googling "Motley Crue Theater of Pain" to show them what it is. I keep pointing at his ankle to get the message across.

No one from the embassy accompanies me to the police department, not a soul. Even Ahtziri could not come with me. They seem to have no grasp of English. The police ask Yadira about the phone being off the hook, and she translates, "They want to know why the phone was off the hook." I explain, "Because I woke up, and my husband was dead. I was frantic, screaming. What would you do?" I tell them the hotel operator said for me to stay on the phone until the doctor arrived, and as far as I knew, I'd hung the phone up when he arrived.

The police inform me that they didn't find any sharp objects or puncture wounds, no broken glass, or marks on Ross. As if they are trying to frame me for his death, I fear that they might accuse me of something. At that point, the big guy leaves the room. He eventually returns, handing me Ross's wedding ring. Yadira asks me to confirm that it's his ring, which I do.

Four agonizing hours pass at the police station. I sit there mostly in silence, anxiety gnawing at my insides. Finally, I snap and blurt out, "Is anybody going to tell me how my husband died!?" Without looking up from their desk, they deliver the news: Ross died of a massive heart attack.

Those words set the room on spin cycle. Chaos and confusion overtake me, and I can't stop the never-ending flurry of thoughts bouncing around my head like a pinball. "A heart attack?" I say to myself, "Not a drug overdose? How can this be?" I was so sure he'd died by his own misuse of the very pills meant to help him. Now, this truth is bringing me back to the start, back to where it all began, our hotel.

And that's exactly where Yadira drags me as the fear of a Mexican prison stays behind in that dingy room. When I get back to the hotel, everyone hugs me and prays with me. The bellmen have become my family. Yadira tells me, "If you want Ross cremated, we can do it tonight, and you can have his ashes tomorrow."

Yadira explains that the fee is just $1,700 and includes the cremation service, death certificates from Mexico, the urn box and associated fees.

She then asks if I want to see Ross before the cremation, and I say yes. She tells me she'll be back to get me in a few hours. I tell Ahtziri that I'm going to the pharmacy and plan to record our conversation because I suspect that the medication the pharmacist sold Ross played a role in his death. She warns me that if I do that, I might not go home.

I can't shake the feeling that something is amiss. I continue to persist and tell everyone that nothing can stop me from vindicating Ross. I believe those medications have something to do with his death, and I want to confront the villain in my version of this story. Ahtziri tells me to think of my children and promises me once again that if I go through with my plan, I may never see them again. She pleads with me to wait for the toxicology report to provide answers. I don't want to, but I finally concede.

At 6:00 p.m., Ross is scheduled for cremation. Yadira picks me up at 5:00 p.m., and we go to see Ross. This time, I know where we are going. We arrive at her office so I can pay for the cremation. Unfortunately, they don't accept American Express, my usual card, and my Apple Pay declines due to my traveling status. I try my Verizon credit card, and suddenly, I receive a text alerting me of a suspicious purchase. I realize the absurdity of my credit card company being skeptical of a cremation charge in Mexico. Still, I confirm it's me during a phone call with the credit card company, and the payment goes through. I obtain the receipt and then we drive across the street to see Ross.

As we drive up, I see a metal wall with a tiny door. I can't help but think, "This is where they cremate people. It's insane." Yadira knocks on the door, speaking through a slit in the door, just like in the TV series, Narco Wars. They permit us to enter, and as I walk in, I expect to find something akin to a morgue. Instead, there's a large parking lot with about 15 cars and people washing vehicles in the open air. I find it oddly fitting because Ross always insisted on having a clean car, no matter where we were.

We walk further, and I have to wait outside another open door while Yadira speaks to a man inside. When she signals for me to enter, I expect to be led to a room where they'd ask me to pull out a tray and reveal Ross's body. Instead, it's nothing like that. He's already lying on a gurney, bagged and ready for cremation. They say, "Take as long as you want."

I take the time to talk to him, pray, and take photos. My friend had suggested I take a picture holding his hand, but when I try to unzip the bag, they stop me. Rushing over, they insist I touch nothing. Instead, they take his hand out for me to hold briefly. I'm able to snap a quick photo, something that I cherish to do this day. After about ten minutes, I leave the room, and they escort me back to the hotel, assuring me I'll likely have his ashes by noon the following day.

That night, Ahtziri encourages me to go down to the ocean and talk to God. She says the ocean will bring healing. I thank God for sending me all my angels, as everyone at the resort has become like family to me. Every morning and night, I still walk by the ocean, a comforting routine that helps me cope.

By the water, I find peace. I feel Ross all around me, healing me. Urging me to keep moving like he always did.

The next morning is Sunday, and Reed is texting me that I need to get some cash. He suggests that I give all the people at the resort something for all of their help and that I need cash to come home with.

It's as if I've gained a sense of invincibility. I mean, they didn't arrest me, my husband's gone—what else can life throw at me? So I decide to venture out. I'm stopped right away by my friends at the bellman's desk asking me where I think I'm going to walk to. I respond,""I need cash and your ATM is out, and I have to get some money." They protest, "You're not going alone," but I'm determined. "No way, it's just a mile down to Walmart. I'll walk."

By the time I grab my things from the room, my friend from Canada, Nelson, who visits Cabo every year, has already been alerted by the bellmen. They tell me that Nelson is on his way up. "What?" I exclaim. "Yes. Nelson has arranged an Uber for you," they inform me. "And he's coming with you." I insist, "He doesn't have to. I just need cash." But they're adamant, "You're not going off this resort alone."

Nelson's wife Shelley stays by the pool while we go on a mission to find cash. We end up visiting three different ATMs because I want to thank the resort staff for their help.

Back at the hotel, before I can lose my nerve, I open up my Facebook account to write the hardest post of my life. It's January 28th, 2023, and I must tell all my extended friends and family that Ross is dead:

It is with a very broken heart and tears in my eyes to let everyone know heaven received my angel yesterday! Ross/Chico was my best friend, a wonderful husband that only wanted what was best for Eli Wolff, Zach Wolff and Noah Wolff! He stepped right into my crazy life of a mom of 3 boys, 16 years ago and never looked back. He had the biggest heart of anyone I know and of course the most stubborn person I have ever known! His smile melts my heart! I love you today, tomorrow, and always! You passed away in our most favorite place on earth, Cabo! I am blessed by God to have a whole new family from everyone at the resort!

God took the love of my life that no one will ever replace but God knows what he is doing!

My love until we see each other again I will always love you and laugh when I see things that remind me of you!

I Love you with all my heart and soul!

I get through that night, and the following day is when I receive Ross's remains.

Fourteen months later, I'm still awaiting that toxicology report. The death certificate simply states the cause of death: a massive heart attack, attributed to obesity and high blood pressure. I have no choice but to question myself, wondering if I was wrong all along. Did his heart essentially give out or was it the unprescribed pain pills from a Mexican pharmacy, or the COVID vaccine. I will never know!

I finally receive Ross's remains and head down to the ocean. I place the box on my blanket and start talking to him. Passersby probably think I'm losing it, but I look up to the sky with hope in my heart that he's in heaven. Even though I know he had a deep relationship with God, I look for confirmation. So, I silently pray, "God, show me a sign. Let me know." I gaze up at the clouds, and there it is—a sign. It looks like a finger pointing up to heaven. I capture it in a photo.

Keeping that a secret between me, God and Ross, I take a moment to update my friends and family back home with another Facebook post:

I have had many questions from friends on what happened! I was informed yesterday that he died of a massive heart attack, and he didn't hurt as it took him very fast as we slept!

As I have been here in Cabo trying to get everything sorted out in a foreign country this has led me to a new family that I will love forever and will always have a place in my heart! The staff at Villa Del Palmar Resort & Spa (Cabo, Mexico) has opened their hearts and faith and friendship to me! Those of you know how much you mean to me! I couldn't walk by the amazing bellman without one of them to stop what they were doing to give me a hug and truly want to know how I am doing! Taking time to pray with me and encouraging words constantly! I cannot even show my gratitude to each one of you! I look forward to continuing our family connection!

As well as my friends Nelson Chmuhalek and Shelly Chmuhalek! By chance to meet in the hot tub by just talking which is what I do best, you have opened your hearts to me and made sure I was safe at all times! Even though it was hard to accept your help I can't thank you enough!

As hard as this has been on me and my family it wasn't without the hand of God in every second giving me strength that I needed to be strong and now have what I need to go home!

If you are reading this know that this world is full of more generous loving people than what we see on the news and negative people talking. I am a witness to the love God has for all his children everywhere on earth!

I am excited to get home, but I want to let everyone know how much you mean to me and having the chance to cry and laugh remembering my dear husband, dad, son, brother, uncle, friend and coworker! We are all better because of Ross/Chico! He brought out the best in all of us!

Thanks again for the thoughts and prayers I have felt from the moment this nightmare started!

I will be working with our families to set a date for everyone to come and celebrate this amazing man that I was lucky enough to call my husband for 14 years!

I am sending my love and gratitude to everyone!

Like I told everyone it's not goodbye but until we see each other again!

Tears start streaming down my face, and a profound sense of peace washes over me, like nothing I've ever felt before. That night, with his remains on my nightstand, I let my emotions flow. I cry and cry, yearning for someone to hold me and reassure me that everything will be okay.

After days of grappling with this alone, I lay down, and as I doze off, I feel a presence—someone holding me. I'm convinced it's God. It was the most peaceful night's sleep I've ever experienced. I actually slept through the entire night, wrapped in a sense of serenity that defies explanation. I literally feel a hand and a presence beside me all night.

Chapter 3

Navigating Grief and Financial Chaos

Lean on, trust in, and be confined to the Lord with all your heart and mind and do not rely on your own insight or understanding.

~Proverbs 3:5

It's Sunday now, three days since Ross died. I'm still at the resort, waiting to be able to leave and go home. It's a strange feeling because I want to go home for my kids, but at the same time, even though Ross is coming home with me, it's a different kind of homecoming. I am almost afraid to face reality. Even though I know it's real, up until now I've been focused on all the phone calls I had to make that Friday—having to call everybody and retell the story, all while trying to hold back tears. It was real to me, but I was also at peace.

It's like I'm trying to protect my sanity and emotions by staying here in Cabo. I don't want anything to change because what if making changes brings more hurt?

Ahtziri warns me that I can't stop pain from coming. She says, "You need to realize something. When you go home, you're going to be starting from scratch." She tells me that these days in Mexico have been to process what happened and figure out how to move forward. Everybody back home knows what's going on, but it won't fully register for them until you return.

This turns out to be true, and it was quite overwhelming.

When I walk in the door that Monday night, all I can do is cry. I'm worried because I still have a child at home, and I don't know how we are going to make it. Noah's first question to me that night is, "Are we going to be able to stay in our house?" I look at him and promise that we will find a way.

Moving from our home is the last thing I want to do, which makes dealing with bills and funeral expenses my highest priority. I know that Ross has life insurance, but where it is and how to get it is a mystery to me. The stack of mail waiting on the counter for me is my first mountain to tackle, but I can't seem to make it past the sea of family waiting to take me into their arms.

They usher me off to bed, and just before I collapse, my eyes well up with fresh tears, reading a post from my sweet son Noah:

"I love you, Ross. I may not have been your biological child but you made me feel like I was one. You raised me for 16 years of my life and I never was able to show you how much I appreciated you. I appreciate the person you have turned me into. Thank you for everything you have ever done for me. I hope you are resting well."

I wake on Tuesday with renewed focus. I have to sort everything out. My parents are with me at the house, having driven to be with my kids. We sit down to address the mail. In one envelope, I find a check for $60,000 labeled as a retirement fund and a letter saying that our account is officially closed.

My heart begins to race as I flash back to the week before Cabo. Ross is telling me that he needs to take a bit more money out of our retirement savings. He doesn't offer an amount, and I don't ask. I never give it much thought. He's always mentioning our retirement account. Either his plans to take money out or his plans to put it all back once he lands a better job. I just let the words go in one ear and out the other. I trust he knows what he's doing and figure we have at least a hundred thousand dollars to work with anyway.

The letter I'm holding that reads "account closed" snaps me back to reality, and it's like a punch to the throat.

I think, "Oh my goodness, now I don't have a retirement account." My dad rushes to my side. He says we need to take inventory.

I tell him I know the cars are paid off, but not the mortgage. I'm filled with dread trying to think of who I pay for that. Where is that information? It's the last thing I want to worry about. "Ross has always taken care of all the bills," I tell my dad. "Most everything is in his name." Fortunately, I recall that my name is on the house. However, his name is the only name on all four vehicles, including the kids' cars. Even the utilities are in his name.

I realize that I need to access our financial records, but Ross has organized everything electronically. I don't know how to get into his phone, his computer, or the safe. We can't locate any files or documents, and I'm completely stuck.

With my son Eli by my side, he reminds me that true to Ross's caretaker nature, before we left, he wrote down the life insurance policy details. Eli recounts him saying, "I don't think you'll need these, but just in case, here's your mom's life insurance. And here's my life insurance."

Eli runs and grabs the piece of paper and I see where my beloved Ross has scrawled the names of our life insurers—State Farm and General Life—down. I immediately call State Farm, only to find out that I can't proceed without the death certificate from the embassy. My mind races, unsure of how I'll ever cover the funeral expenses, as I hear my dad suggesting our next step.

"Why don't you go to the police department and see if they can hack into Ross's computer."

It sounds like a better idea to me than panicking, so we load it up and head to the Eagan police department. Walking in, I feel the weight of all eyes on me. As I describe my predicament to the detective standing behind the counter, I see warmth in his eyes and says, "Let me see what we can do." He takes Ross's computer and heads to the back of the precinct. Moments later, he returns with a frown on his face and says, "I wish I could help. But it turns out there's nothing we can do. Because we're unsure of whether a crime has been committed, we're not able to do anything."

Back home, Eli, being tech-savvy, jumps in to help. Right away, he's able to access some of Ross's emails. However, we can't retrieve everything we need. Then it dawns on me, "Oh my gosh, the guy at Computer Tech set up Ross's computer." I decide to give them a call, although it's been years since we last spoke. When he answers, I say, "I'm not sure if you remember me, but you helped my husband Ross when he worked for MedCare." He recalls and agrees to assist. He tells me, "Bring it in. I can't promise results but let me see what I can do."

I take the computer in and he manages to access it, but he doesn't go too far since delving too deep might risk losing everything. At least we can find some files on it, but still, there's nothing related to any of the household expenses.

My dad and I begin the manual process of printing off all my bank statements to search for payments made and to whom. Then I start making phone calls, retelling my story numerous times, trying not to break down.

Most of the time, it's a straightforward process when dealing with the service providers. They help me to simply switch the accounts into my name, making it relatively easy.

For some financial matters, like the mortgage, I have to wait until I receive the US death certificate from the embassy. The process is complex and time-consuming. Ross's brother Reed helps us because his best friend, Donnie, did our mortgage. We learn that we need to talk to the title company to get Ross's name removed from the house. When I talk to the title company, they assure me that once they have a copy of the death certificate, they will switch the house into my name.

I face more difficulties at the bank because all payments are automatically set up under Ross's name, and we need to change them. However, because of his death and concerns about fraud, the bank temporarily stops all payments from the accounts. I spend hours at the bank trying to figure out the next steps.

The funeral costs remain a significant concern. My portion comes to $5,500, while Ross's brother, Reed, steps in to graciously cover the expenses for obituaries so they can be published in three different papers. I'm not aware of the exact cost, but I know obituaries are more expensive than one might think. For instance, when we had to place one for Ross's father, it cost around $800 for a single obituary, with just a photo. My own expenses continue to mount as my son's car needs repair, adding another $2,500 to the growing pile of bills.

Barry, Ross's other brother, gives me $1,000 to assist with the funeral costs, and Reed lends me $3,000, knowing it will be a long wait for the life insurance payout.

Planning the Ceremony

In the midst of all this stress, and with my brain in a fog, I meet with the church to plan the funeral. I feel the financial burden hanging over me as credit card debt piles up by the second. It is a challenging time, and my dad, who has a strong financial background, tries to assist me while we start official plans for the service.

The morning Ross died, I had called my close friend and pastor, Chad, so I already know he will be officiating the celebration of life. I remember him telling me to just take each day one day at a time, and I'm trying. Sitting in my church though, waiting to talk with Lisa who arranges funerals, I realize this is one day I certainly don't want to take.

My parents and mother-in-law, Sandie, are here with me, and so is Eli. He worked in production at the church, and I know he'll help me make all the right decisions. I keep going in and out of a warm fog that has somehow become my ever-present companion. Lisa is asking who should sing. I look at Eli and say, "Aaron," I remember how much Ross loved to listen to him sing. "That will be wonderful," I say to no one in particular.

"Who will be speaking?" Lisa asks next. "Oh boy," I think. If only Ross was here to guide me through this one. Everyone has their pick of who should offer eulogies. We spoke at length about this the night I returned from Mexico. Such a delicate situation and my people-pleasing tendencies came out with a vengeance.

I still want everyone happy, and it seems hurt feelings are inevitable. My dad really wants to speak, but he doesn't want to step on anyone's toes. Sandie, of course, has her feelings and thoughts about who should speak as well. And me? Well, I couldn't care less. All I know is the only person I want to hear from won't be speaking. "Ross," I say silently. "It's like I'm planning our wedding, only you, my groom, have left the building."

I'm on pins and needles as I recite the list of speakers to Lisa, hoping and praying it's inclusive enough and respectful of everyone's feelings.

Sandi Walhof, Ross's mom. Nathan Tubergren, my dad and John Draxter, Ross's good friend.

Lisa then asks about the scriptures and songs we want read, played, and performed. This is something I actually care about, so I pipe up. "I want to focus on the fact that worrying won't change anything," I say. "This is a message that Ross and I often shared during the last year of his life, and it's important to me."

My mom, who knows the Bible inside and out, starts throwing out verse and verse. But no matter what she offers, I keep coming back to Matthew 6-25-27.

[25] "Therefore I tell you, do not worry about your life, what you will eat or drink; or about your body, what you will wear. Is not life more than food, and the body more than clothes? [26] Look at the birds of the air; they do not sow or reap or store away in barns, and yet your heavenly Father feeds them. Are you not much more valuable than they? [27] Can any one of you by worrying add a single hour to your life[a]?

Finally, my mom says, "Candy, if that's it, then that's what it is."

It's decided that we should have Ava, Ross's brother's daughter, read the verse. I check with Sandie to see if she's willing to do it, and she agrees.

Then, my neighbor from across the street, whose children grew up with mine, suggests having an open mic for people to share their memories and thoughts. I'm not sure if anyone will speak up, but she's confident that Noah, her son, might. Noah, often nicknamed "Mr. President" for his intelligence, used to engage in debates with Ross.

We set the date for the *ceremony*; I mean funeral. February 16, 2023, at Crossroads Church at the Woodbury campus, Pastor Chad Melton will usher my husband into his final resting place, heaven.

Aaron will sing "Home," and I ask that they play "Scars in Heaven" by Casting Crowns. Every time I hear those lyrics, even before losing Ross, I can't help but sing.

The only scars in Heaven, they won't belong to me and you

There'll be no such thing as broken, and all the old will be made new

And the thought that makes me smile now, even as the tears fall down

Is that the only scars in Heaven are on the hands that hold you now

Ross was hurting so much on earth, but in heaven, he is healed.

The other song we'll play, at Rich's request, is "Eagles Fly" by Sammy Hagar. We all love Sammy so much. In fact, Ross always teased me that Kenny Chesney and Sammy Hagar were my boyfriends. We knew that Ross would love that song to be played.

We leave the church well aware that we need to address the life insurance. Without the US death certificate, there is very little we can do. It's incredibly frustrating. The holdup with the death certificate seems to be related to the fact that we don't have our marriage certificate with us in Mexico, so they can only list Ross as single. I have to provide additional documentation, including our marriage certificate and my birth certificate and his birth certificate for the embassy to process the death certificate.

Still, it's a big waiting game. I reach out to my State Farm representative. He confirms again that we must wait for the certified death certificate before they can proceed. They promise a check in five to seven days once they have the death certificate. This proves problematic.

With Ross passing away in a foreign country, it brings the difficulty to a whole new level. The whole process involves multiple levels, including the need to submit a investigator's report back to State Farm. They must first find someone in the local area to go to the police station, funeral home, and crematory to verify the paperwork, then submit the report back to State Farm. It's an uncertain waiting game. All the documentation is in Spanish and needs to be translated.

While State Farm is the primary life insurance, we also have a policy with General Life Insurance. I call them, hoping for a quicker resolution, but they direct me to fill out the paperwork *after* I obtain the certified death certificate. However, obtaining this document is entirely reliant on the embassy's timeline, so I can't move forward. I don't have an agent with General Life, so I must handle all of that on my own.

As I'm trying to make sense of the bills and get my name on as many accounts as possible. On top of all this, I have to go to the Mayo Clinic for my fifth surgery. It was scheduled prior to Ross's death, and I wanted to cancel it, but my dad insists that I still have it as that is what Ross would want. My dad goes with me to help and that night, in the hotel, one week after the loss of my husband, we start making a financial plan.

We go through all the bills, both the information given over the phone and what we found on our own. Ross, the wonderful planner he was, had been overpaying bills. Something I learned when I contacted the electric company, for example. He'd paid so much that I had a significant credit, which was a relief. For the first couple of months, I didn't have to worry much about making that payment.

My dad and I calculate all the household bills to be $8,500 a month. With my monthly income of around $5,000 a month, we speculate about the potential income from Social Security and realize I have a shortfall.

Having a $60,000 cash out from 401(k) provides some relief, giving me a buffer while I work out the details. Still, the stress of not knowing about everything else is frustrating, and my immediate response is to wander back through my marriage to Ross.

Since marrying him, the only bill I ever paid was our cell phone. Other than that, I bought groceries. Ross took care of everything else. This was the norm throughout our marriage—he had a traditional mindset where he believed it was his role to provide for the family financially. He took care of the outside responsibilities and paid the bills. When I worked, I contributed to the kids' expenses, but he often contributed extra money when he could. My job essentially covered expenses related to the kids, like their clothes, school supplies, field trips, and lunch money.

Initially, Ross and I had about $400,000 in our 401(k). Ross started borrowing against our 401(k) when he lost job, and this went on since 2018. Losing his job was already a hit to his identity because he defined himself through his work. He had always been successful, both financially and professionally, and he took pride in being the provider for our family. He didn't want me to work; he wanted me to have the freedom to do whatever I wanted and to take care of the kids.

When he first lost his job, he received a severance, and then there was unemployment for some time. I also took a second job right away at Nordstrom to gain health insurance.

I was already working part-time for a company called Innovative, as an independent contractor, where I planned corporate trips. Ross gave me a figure I needed to make each month, which only required me to work 20 hours a month, so it was a good balance.

Ross, however, struggled to find a way back into the medical field, primarily because they tend to hire younger people. He took a sales role at a manufacturing company, but he'd only been there four months when COVID hit. The job market crashed. He lost his job, and I lost mine.

Even after COVID, the job market didn't favor Ross. By the time he could reenter the workforce, he had been out of work for several years and was getting older.

I knew he was dipping into the 401(k), but I wasn't aware of the exact amount because he handled our finances, including our children's 529 plans. At one point, he mentioned there were still a couple of hundred thousand dollars left in the 401(k). It didn't concern me too much at the time. I thought he would eventually find another job, and we still had time to rebuild the savings. This was about five years ago when I was 45 and he was 50. It seemed like there were plenty of working years ahead.

Sadly, today I'm facing a different reality. I have no retirement, and only life insurance to provide a buffer.

Ross's reluctancy to share details about the finances was his way of not worrying me. He always felt responsible for providing. Whenever I would ask about the bills, he would just say, "Don't worry about it," and I never questioned him.

Now that he's gone, I have no choice but to question myself.

How did I let this happen? Why am I here alone with nothing but a pile of bills and bits and pieces of information about my family's household expenses.

If only I had more time to analyze it all, but I don't. I need to plan my husband's funeral.

The Funeral

The days leading up to the service are spent compiling photo boards. My house is filled with family, friends, and neighbors sorting through pictures. We create about nine picture boards, which prompt both laughter and tears as we reminisce about our journey together. It's heartwarming to revisit all the good memories, the places we've been, and the experiences we've shared.

As I'm shifting through photos on my desk. I come across the Mexican death certificate. I've maybe read it 15 times already, but that doesn't stop my eyes from scanning over its contents again. I read through the cause of death: massive heart attack and high blood pressure.

I ask myself again, did this happen because of the fentanyl epidemic? Were the pain pills he bought in Mexico laced with fentanyl? Or could it have been the COVID vaccines? Or was it truly just a heart attack? I still have so many unanswered questions.

I doubt the Mexican police will ever release the toxicology report to me. While I want proof that the OxyContin he bought was not laced with fentanyl, I truly believe, in my heart, they don't want anyone to know there is a fentanyl-lacing epidemic spurred by the Mexican drug cartels.

It wasn't until I was back in the states that I learned the drug cartels run all the pharmacies in Mexico. Naïve of me, I know. Still, there was the one pharmacy that was actually honest with us. So many uncertainties, so many unanswered questions that I just have to place my faith in God.

Do I know for certain that my husband was in pain mentally, physically, emotionally? Yes, he was. Do I know he's in a better place? Yes, I do. Do I miss him every day? Yes! But we live life forward and learn by looking backward. And I truly believe from what my dear friend Debbie told me, that with the heart attack Ross had, he went quick. He wasn't in pain, and even if I would have woken up and heard anything, or I would have had doctors there when it happened, nobody would have been able to do anything to save him. It was simply his time.

I remember now that Debbie also said that with this kind of heart attack that Ross had, you usually have signs about 5 days prior of some sort of warning that something is going on. That's when it hits me! I grab my phone and start searching for the selfie he and I took at Cabo Wabo. That photo, which turned out to be the last picture of us together, is nestled safely in my iPhone photo album. To my shock, I see that Ross looks gray. It's almost as if his body is already failing, the days before he died.

I feel fresh tears welling up in my eyes as I realize I hadn't noticed his appearance being off that day. I knew he was struggling, but the look of death in his own eyes had escaped me. He was very tired and complained of not feeling well, but did I see those signs? I did not.

I sense this truth might haunt me for days to come. But just like every other aspect of my grief, it proves fleeting.

The thing about grief is it's not black and white; it's every shade of grey. It's possible for you to experience many emotions at the exact same time. You can go from being completely undone to feeling fine. Since the day I woke up and found Ross dead, everything in my life has been chaotic, crazy, and mixed up. Some days are good, and some days I have no idea what's happening or how I'll ever survive. But every day, I remind myself that I made it through the day—I am ok and tomorrow's a new day.

I have learned to live in the present moment and let whatever emotion I'm having simply hit me. As many friends have advised me, to give myself grace.

Noah has just informs me that Amazon has just delivered a package. So, I let him tell me the baby urns I've ordered for Ross's ashes have arrived. I embrace the sweetness that he's displayed in this whole process of how to preserve Ross. He insisted on getting necklaces for everybody to house their portion of ashes. He chose a hockey stick pendant for himself and others for the boys, Ross's mom, and Rich, his best friend.

It takes me time throughout the day, but I finally muster the courage to open the box containing Ross's ashes from Cabo and fill those necklaces. Roxy, our dog, is with me. She adored Ross, and when I reach for the box, she immediately senses something's wrong. Despite the ashes being an inanimate object, I watch her run straight to her kennel, lie down, and let out a loud cry. It breaks my heart, but I think she knows Ross isn't coming home.

Looking back to the box, I see what looks like a Ziplock bag inside. "Wonderful," I think. "I'll just open that up and pour the ashes into the new urn."

As I do this, I realize these ashes are different than any I've seen before. They're not fine and powdery like typical cremains. These ashes are grey with little chunks of bone.

I guess I should be horrified, but I'm not. I'm just trying to figure out how to portion them into the mini urn necklaces. The dilemma is real—I can't fathom using a regular spoon, the kind we eat with every day, to handle my deceased husband's ashes. So, I start rummaging through various items and stumble upon a plastic Dairy Queen Blizzard spoon. "That's the ticket," I say out loud.

It strikes me as somewhat poetic, possibly even one that Ross has used, given his love for Heath Dairy Queen Blizzards. So, I start scooping ashes from the urn into the necklaces. I plan to toss that spoon afterward, as I can't imagine using it for anything else!

My mom is with me, and it takes about an hour to fill all the necklaces. I end up with ashes all over me. A few days later, as I'm recounting the story to Ross's mom, she says, "Even when he's gone, he's still all over you." We laugh so hard we cry.

On the eve of my husband's funeral, I stumble upon a picture from our trip to St. Martin. Journaling to my Facebook family, I write, "I miss him so much and know tomorrow will be the hardest day of my life! I am feeling blessed to know I will be surrounded by family and friends to celebrate Ross/Chico in a way that is only fitting for my one-of-a-kind husband! Love you babe forever and ever!"

That night, I talk to Rich, Ross's best friend, quite a bit. He reminds me that there will be so many people at the funeral that I don't know. Being Ross's best friend and uncle to the kids, he promises to be by my side the whole time and introduce me to everyone.

The church is large and full, a somewhat unexpected turnout. Although Ross grew up in White Bear, he'd lost touch with many of his old friends when he moved to Arizona. He wasn't able to make it back to any of the reunions, and time with friends was often limited. Despite that, a multitude of people show up, many of whom I don't even know. Rich is true to his word, staying by my side and making all the introductions.

I see a gorgeous picture of Ross on the funeral program everyone is carrying. I grab one for myself and begin reading. Pastor Chad will offer a welcome and a prayer. Then Aaron will sing "Home." Pastor Chad will read the poem, "To My Dearest Family." Sandie, Nathan, and John will speak, and then they'll play the heartfelt songs I picked. "Wonderful," I think as tears start spilling down my cheeks.

Ross WALHOF Obituary

Age 55 of Eagan, MN Passed away January 27, 2023 Loving Husband, Dad, Son, Brother, Uncle, Cousin, Nephew and friend. Preceded in death by his father, Erv Walhof. Survived by his loving wife, Candy (Wolff), and three sons, Zach (Shelbi), Eli and Noah

Wolff; his mother, Sandra Walhof and younger brothers Barry and Reed (Kelley), niece Ava and nephew Charlie. Ross (affectionately nicknamed Chico) lived life loud and full of passion. A 1986 graduate of White Bear Lake High School, Ross later attended the University of River Falls, WI. He enjoyed a long career in medical sales. Chico was the ultimate salesperson. Given his infectious smile, quick wit and cheerful attitude, customers enjoyed buying from him. He exhibited abundant energy and loved to work with his hands. He assisted many friends with building projects. He enjoyed watching and playing sports, especially hockey, but his true love was college football! He loved rock music & 80's hair bands. He & Candy enjoyed traveling, especially to their happy place, Cabo San Lucas. Ross loved the outdoors and was an avid hunter. He created great memories with the Van Hulzen cousins as well as family in Edgerton, MN. He spent hours reminiscing and telling stories of many memorable past events with cousins and friends. Chico will be missed but not forgotten! Service will be held on Thursday, February 16 at Crossroads Church, 5900 Woodbury Drive, Woodbury, MN. 9:30-11AM visitation and service at 11AM. In lieu of flowers, donations preferred to the American Heart Assoc. or The Michael J. Fox Parkinson's Foundation.
Published by Pioneer Press on Feb. 5, 2023.

I see friends, coworkers, and even neighbors filling the sanctuary. Brooks Smith, friend and my former boss, approaches me. He gives me a knowing look as I flash back to Ross and I comforting him just eight weeks ago when he lost his wife, Jennifer. He leans in for a hug, and I hear him say, "You won't remember who's here or who you speak to." This puts me instantly at ease, and the burden of hosting this awful event lightens, if only for a moment.

Pastor Chad is praying now. I bow my head and think of Ross. If wishes could come true, he'd be sitting here with me now. Instead, I'm mourning his loss and closing my eyes.

Aaron begins to sing.

"This world is not what it was meant to be, all this pain, all this suffering, there's a better place waiting for me in Heaven."

I see Ross now. I know he's in Heaven.

"Every tear will be wiped away. Every sorrow and sin erased. We'll dance on seas of amazing grace. In Heaven. In Heaven. I'm goin' home. Where the streets are golden.

Every chain is broken. Oh I wanna go. Oh I wanna go. Home. Where every fear is gone. I'm in your open arms. Where I belong. Home."

We're all crying and consoling each other when Pastor Chad addresses us again, "To My Dearest Family."

Oh yes! It's the poem that Eli and I found in the safe after Ross had passed. A prophetic word perhaps or just a last-minute love note, either way, I sense his presence here with us today.

Some things I'd like to say,
but first of all to let you know
that I arrived okay
I'm writing this from Heaven
where I dwell with God above
where there's no more tears
or sadness there
is just eternal love
Please do not be unhappy
just because I'm out of sight
remember that I'm with you
every morning, noon and night
That day I had to leave you
when my life on Earth was through
God picked me up and hugged me
and He said I welcome you
It's good to have you back again
you were missed while you were gone
as for your dearest family
they'll be here later on
I need you here so badly
as part of My big plan

there's so much that we have to do
to help our mortal man
Then God gave me a list of things
He wished for me to do
and foremost on that list of mine
is to watch and care for you
And I will be beside you
every day and week and year
and when you're sad
I'm standing there
to wipe away the tear
And when you lie in bed at night
the days chores put to flight
God and I are closest to you
in the middle of the night
When you think of my life on Earth
and all those loving years
because you're only human
they are bound to bring you tears
But do not be afraid to cry
it does relieve the pain
remember there would be no flowers
unless there was some rain
I wish that I could tell you
of all that God has planned
but if I were to tell you
you wouldn't understand

But one thing is for certain
though my life on Earth is over
I am closer to you now
than I ever was before
And to my very many friends
trust God knows what is best
I'm still not far away from you
I'm just beyond the crest
There are rocky roads ahead of you
and many hills to climb
but together we can do it
taking one day at a time
It was always my philosophy
and I'd like it for you too
that as you give unto the World
so the World will give to you
If you can help somebody
who is in sorrow or in pain
then you can say to God at night
my day was not in vain
And now I am contented
that my life it was worthwhile
knowing as I passed along the way
I made somebody smile
So if you meet somebody
who is down and feeling low
just lend a hand to pick him up

as on your way you go
When you are walking
down the street
and you've got me on your mind
I'm walking in your footsteps
only half a step behind
And when you feel the gentle breeze
or the wind upon your face
that's me giving you a great big hug
or just a soft embrace
And when it's time for you to go
from that body to be free
remember you're not going
you are coming here to me
And I will always love you
from that land way up above
Will be in touch again soon
P.S. God sends His Love
~Author Unknown

Next, Ross's good friend John takes the stage. In an instant, I'm transported back to the first time I met John and his fiancé—come to find out she had no idea that Ross was his real name. We had just arrived at John's house for a visit. I was talking with his fiancé telling her that Ross had slept on the plane. She looked perplexed and said, "Ross? That's his name? I thought his name was Chico!"

We all got a good laugh as we talked about how his nickname Chico came about. His dad Erv was a huge sports fan and one of his favorite players was a man named Chico. So, when Ross was born, Erv called him Chico. The funny thing is Ross looked Mexican with a full head of dark, thick hair. So, from the time he was born, he only went by Chico.

Many people had no idea that his name was Ross. To this day, I go back and forth. When I'm with his family I call him Chico. When I'm with my family or friends, he's Ross.

I hear John struggling to keep from crying and snap back to the present day. He's telling us how he wishes Axl Rose could be speaking instead. He reminisces about how much more fun this would all be if Chico were here. He talks of their fun times growing up and living in Colorado being ski bums, and how he once nearly died from a heart condition, but Chico saved him by calling 911 and was with him the entire time in the hospital.

He shares the pact that they once made: "When I call you, you pick up!"

After my dad and Ross's mom have spoken, Noah, a.k.a. Mr. President, takes the stage. What's remarkable is that most of the guests don't know him. As he speaks about Ross and their unique friendship, he sobs, shedding nonstop light onto who Ross was. His heartfelt and unscripted speech moves everyone, offering a perspective on Ross that no one else could provide.

He tells the room how much Ross loved""Let there be rock" by ACDC, "Love Gun" by KISS, and "Asshole" by Dennis Leery. He confesses that Ross is smiling down on us because Ross always wanted to hear what was on Noah's mind and what he had to say.

As we adjourn, my son Zach is a godsend, making sure that people don't overwhelm me. Despite a constant stream of sad faces appearing before my eyes, his voice intervenes.

"Mom, we need to talk to this person now."

"Mom, it's time to eat."

He takes on the role of a protective companion, ensuring that I'm not pulled in too many directions.

Rightfully so because I'd dropped maybe 20 pounds since Ross died and everyone is worried about me. I barely have an appetite and can never bring myself to eat without being forced. It's strange how grief can affect your basic instincts like hunger and eating.

We are all so exhausted after the funeral. Everyone is standing by the flowers and the food. We have to decide who's taking what. It sounds ridiculous now, but we divvied up the food by sending the desserts home with Sandie and the sandwiches with us. It feels surreal. All I can think is, "Did this really happen?"

Chapter 4

The Aftermath

We may throw the dice, but the Lord determines how they fall.
~Proverbs 16:33

When you wake up one day and your spouse is gone, your whole world changes in an instant. All the security and comfort you once had are no longer there. You're not only dealing with the loss, but you're suddenly responsible for the financial well-being of your family. And it can be incredibly overwhelming, especially if you've never had to manage these responsibilities before.

In my previous marriage, I managed the bills. I was responsible for handling all the financial aspects, from paying the bills to keeping track of our financial situation. When Ross and I first got married, we both contributed financially; I even gave him around $500 a month to help with rent. It was a manageable arrangement.

However, as he started earning more, he took on the responsibility and told me not to worry about it. At that time, my dad probably thought I had everything under control since I'd been through it before and seemed capable of handling our finances. But going from a position of having everything you want and not stressing about money to a point where you're struggling and seeking assistance from a food bank is quite a journey. It's remarkable how you adapt to your circumstances.

When we were financially comfortable, I often wondered why we weren't saving more. To his credit, Ross did invest wisely. For instance, we managed to pay off our cars by cashing out Netflix stocks he'd bought on a whim when he lost his job. It provided a financial cushion for a while.

He was smart with our finances, doing everything right up to the point where he couldn't find a job that matched his expectations. He'd put in the effort, had exceptional sales skills, and could sway people's perspectives with ease. He built strong relationships in his sales career and was truly outstanding at it. It was disheartening when he couldn't secure a job despite being highly skilled and knowledgeable.

As our savings dwindled and bills piled up, he didn't want me to worry about our financial situation. So, he started taking money out of our retirement. This was in the early days of COVID, and I know he intended to put it all back when he got a new job. He just ran out of time. And now I have to go on alone. I have to find a way to support myself and my teenage son.

The funeral is over, and reality sends me to Social Security. The agent I speak with informs me that because Ross didn't work for the last year and a half of his life, I won't be receiving any benefits.

They tell me I will eventually have access to widow's benefits, which can be claimed starting at ages 60. For now, they're issuing me a check for $255, which is the full death benefit for a spouse.

However, after speaking to friends, I realize that Social Security benefits are calculated based on a person's entire working history, not just their recent income. I also wonder if our youngest son, Noah, who is under the age of 18, might be eligible for benefits.

As my frustration mounts, I file an appeal with Social Security, having gathered all the documentation to prove my case. It's a significant undertaking, and I realize that when someone passes away, you must become your own advocate. As I delve into the details, I learn that Ross's biological connection to Noah is irrelevant to receiving Social Security benefits, thank goodness. Still, this is something I never would have known on my own. And clarity seems to be missing in all these challenging, bureaucratic processes.

As for Noah, being under 18, he still qualifies for certain benefits. However, I have to compose a substantial rebuttal, and even though the agent promises to call me back, he never does. I have to track him down myself and eventually he confirms that Noah indeed qualifies. He apologizes for the lack of communication, and I learn yet another lesson in advocating for myself rather than waiting forever for help that doesn't come.

Unfortunately, that good news goes sour when Noah is officially denied benefits. I must submit another rebuttal attempting to prove that Ross supported Noah at 50% for the last years of his life.

I must present several documents to Social Security, including Noah's birth certificate, our marriage certificates, tax returns from the past year, and child support documents. While they require the original paper copies, I opt to hand deliver them and request that copies be made. I am told to expect a response within 45 days. However, before that timeframe can lapse, I am denied again and offered one last appeal. And at the publishing of this book, fourteen months after Ross's death, I still have no official word on Noah's eligibility.

If he does qualify, they'll likely retroactively pay from the time of Ross's death, and his eligibility will continue until he graduates high school. But if he were just a few years younger, I would have been entitled to Social Security benefits as well. It's quite complicated and confusing.

To make matters worse, I also have taxes to contend with, which are a complete mess.

My friend, Brooks, has always handled our taxes, but I had never paid much attention until now. He recommends that I search for any files or documents Ross may have saved over the years. However, I can't find anything. So, he provides me with a list of the required documents.

I scan all the necessary documents and send them over to Brooks for him to work on. Tax Day is quickly approaching, and I must admit I'm quite stressed. I am hesitant to have Brooks complete my taxes until I know I have the financial means to pay the amount due. I'm concerned because Brooks tells me that there would be tax penalties for withdrawing funds from the 401(k). We already paid a significant amount in taxes the previous year, and I wasn't sure what to expect this time.

As the tax deadline approaches, my nerves are shot. Then out of nowhere, I receive a check from General Life for $250,000 and I think, "Okay, now I have the money." So, I meet with Brooks and go over the details. To my surprise, he tells me I have to write a huge check to the federal government. We owe $15,000! They don't offer any kind of widow pass, and I have no choice but to pay it. The fact that Ross passed away in January 2023 means that we would incur another year of penalties due to the last part of his retirement being received in that year. Fortunately, life insurance payouts aren't subject to taxes, so I have all of those funds to pay my taxes and other bills.

Another ongoing issue is my dealings with an attorney who handled Ross's divorce from his first wife. Unfortunately, this attorney has been less than cooperative. Ross had established a payment plan with him, paying $100 monthly until the debt was cleared. However, following Ross's passing, the automatic payments were halted to protect against potential fraudulent attempts to access his accounts. This also meant the attorney stopped receiving payments, which I didn't mind because I had no association with this attorney's services. The arrangement was made long before our marriage, and I had no intention of continuing payments.

Still, I wrote back to the attorney to let him know that Ross had passed away and included a copy of the Mexican death certificate and the US death certificate. I made it clear that he would have to consider this debt as unrecoverable. However, the following month, I received a condolence message acknowledging my loss and demanding $10,000. His letter stated that I wasn't personally responsible for the debt, but rather, Ross's estate would bear this responsibility.

I couldn't help but wonder what kind of attorney lets someone pay only $100 a month against a debt that large. This was his own foolish decision, and I held the attorney responsible for this situation. I responded, reiterating that there is no estate and he shouldn't expect payment.

To my astonishment, the next letter I receive from him says, "I noticed in Ross's obituary that you claimed that you were married to him at the time of his death. However, the certified copy of the death certificate states that he was single." According to him, I wasn't listed under any marriage certification in Minnesota, and Ross was only ever married to Amy, who he had handled the divorce for. He also accuses me of liquidating Ross's retirement, which didn't exist.

This angers me, and I also knew that Ross had already paid the attorney hundreds of thousands of dollars for their divorce, even though their assets at that time were considerably lower.

I clarify in a new letter that Ross has no estate and hasn't been working. I share that I received life insurance only. His response says, "While you yourself are not responsible for the debt of Ross at his death, his estate assets are required by law to be used for debts." The attorney found it hard to believe that Ross hadn't worked for several years before his passing, as he considered Ross a hard worker with a strong work ethic. He also mentioned that Ross had significant assets when he completed his divorce, including three houses, off-road vehicles, snowmobiles, recreational vehicles, and receivables from his mortgage-buying business. He earned over $73,000 from his pharmaceutical job.

This irritates me because Ross never worked in pharmaceuticals. The attorney also states that it is illegal for someone to liquidate another person's retirement assets and asks me to call him.

I discuss this with my brother-in-law, Reed, who is furious with this attorney. He mentions he might have paid the debt to put it behind us. But now, this attorney won't get a dime.

If there is no will and assets need to be distributed, that's when things go through probate and lawyers get involved. Lawyers primarily profit in cases where there are no specified beneficiaries, requiring legal actions to resolve the distribution.

My neighbor advises me not to reply to this attorney again. However, I still receive letters from him, and my neighbor's firm is preparing a letter to stop his harassment.

The most disheartening part, throughout this entire process, was learning that the retirement money was gone, and I'm only 50 years old. I knew I'd eventually receive the life insurance money, and I had a great support system with my mother-in-law, Sandie, brother-in-laws both Reed, and Barry, as well as my parents offering financial help. However, the reality hit hard—that life insurance money has to last me until I die, and I'm only 50. I also have a small 401(k), which is almost negligible for an independent worker.

When asked about assets, I often think about my 401(k), but I only have a few thousand dollars in it. I know how much effort Ross put into planning for our financial future. He had a vision, wanting to have a million dollars in the 401(k), and if he worked ten more years, he believed he could achieve that. We didn't want to rely on Social Security, but he had it all mapped out—the house would be paid off, and we would be set. And now, here I am.

As for the mortgage, I was initially surprised by how low the payments were. I later realized it was because Ross had refinanced to a 15-year mortgage when he had a good job. However, when he lost his job and COVID hit, it must have been very stressful for him. We couldn't refinance because you need a job for that, but fortunately, he managed to get another job after COVID with a healthcare company. It wasn't the best job, but he needed to hold it for three months to refinance our house. The interest rates were at an incredible 2%, so he figured it was a wise decision. He refinanced to a 30-year so payments are small.

To me, financial matters need open discussions, even if someone has a traditional mindset. Since Ross passed, I've spoken to others who realized the importance of these conversations. Many assumed that being married automatically meant shared ownership, but in reality, there are many hoops to jump through to establish legal rights.

Dealing with the death certificate was quite frustrating, as it was held up in Mexico. You want to grieve and handle financial matters simultaneously, but you're at the mercy of bureaucracy. The life insurance situation was another source of frustration. We had been paying premiums for 15 years, and the payout was $250,000. It's not a huge sum, and dealing with the paperwork and waiting periods was exhausting.

Regarding Social Security, the $255 death benefit hasn't changed since its inception, which seems inconsequential today. My attempts to claim benefits for Noah, who is still in school, haven't been straightforward. When your child is over 16, the eligibility for Social Security benefits changes, which can be challenging to navigate. These financial intricacies can be bewildering, especially when you're still raising a child and dealing with the loss of a spouse.

Thankfully, I had discussions with my dad about this. We figured out that I need an additional $20,000 to $30,000 annually to meet all my financial obligations. Right now, I've invested in CDs and money market accounts to ensure I have access to liquid cash while still looking for better investment options.

Looking back, if I'd known better, I would have saved more. I tended to spend recklessly when we had extra money. Seeing all the stuff we accumulated over the years makes me realize that most of it was unnecessary—more importantly, that even the good things in life will not always stay exactly the same because life is always changing.

When I worked for a company that had a 401(k) plan, I should have invested more. Now that I'm managing our finances, I've become more prudent with our spending, especially as I've learned to appreciate the value of financial stability and being prepared.

However, my husband's passing is an eye-opener, a stark reminder that material possessions are just stuff, and when he's not around to enjoy them, they lose their significance. Parting with some of his belongings was hard, but I've found solace in knowing that they've gone to families who truly appreciate them.

I left a lot of Ross's clothes in Mexico and as soon as I was emotionally able, I had a garage sale to offload more of his belongings. This was hard for his mom, Sandie. When I was preparing for the sale, she walked in and saw everything, and it really hit her that he was gone.

Regarding finances, I've learned the importance of transparent discussions. I don't want my parents to experience what I've gone through, so it's essential to start looking at their financial situation comprehensively.

When they pass, it needs to be as easy as possible on everyone.

Had we talked more openly about money and expenses, perhaps we could have made better financial decisions. Sometimes, people mistakenly believe that by protecting their loved ones from financial stress, they're doing them a favor. However, in the long run, this approach can do more harm than good. It's crucial to have open conversations about finances and make decisions as a family. Losing my husband so suddenly is a constant reminder of how life can change in an instant and leave you grappling with that trauma.

Don't let my story be your story. Talk with your partner about the finances. Create a document and store it in a safe that you know the combination for. List out all your account numbers, amounts owed, life insurance policies, and passwords and know who owns and owes what. You don't want to have to figure all this out while grieving.

Chapter 5

Support and Solace

I pray that from his glorious, unlimited resources he will em-
power you with inner strength through his spirit.
~Ephesians 3:16

In the wake of Ross's untimely passing, I find strength and unwavering support from a network that extends far beyond my immediate family. My friends, the pillars of my social foundation, rallied around me during those dark moments when grief threatened to consume me. Their presence became a source of comfort, a reminder that I wasn't navigating this journey alone. Through laughter and countless conversations, I've discovered the profound impact of true friendship.

Equally crucial are the bonds I forged within my family circle. In the face of immense loss, they became a more powerful force than I ever thought possible. My kids, in-laws, parents, and siblings are the silent pillars holding me up, a testament to the endurance of familial ties. Their collective love, shared stories, and buckets of tears have become a sanctuary where I can freely express my grief. And the only beacon of hope I have for the future.

Now that the funeral is over, I'm comforted by the extended presence of my siblings. They've all come to stay with me, sacrificing their own lives, and I take to Facebook to commemorate their visit:

"Donna Scott Tubergen and Nathan Tubergen's love and support has been amazing. Sandra Tiry, Timothy Tubergen, Shawnie Aanstad, Jessica Tiry, Luke Tiry thank you for coming to help me and support me through this hard time! Shelbi Wolff, Eli Wolff, Zach Wolff, and Noah Wolff thanks for being such great kids and keeping an eye on your mom and making sure I eat! I love you guys so much! Sandie Walhof, Kelley Stromberg Walhof, Reed Walhof, Barry Walhof, Ava Walhof, and Charlie Walhof! Thank you for all the love and support as you are grieving as well! I love you guys!!"

It's been one month since Ross died, and I still miss him so much. Being a widow is hard, and I can't figure out my feelings. After my family leaves, I decide to go buy some self-help books. When I get to Barnes & Noble, I literally laugh out loud. The first book I see is entitled, "The Hot Young Widows Club!" I say to myself, "I'm not sure I fit this demographic, but since it makes me laugh, I'm going to buy and read this book."

I must say laughing does feel good! I can only imagine what Ross is saying up in heaven! I suspect he's questioning this purchase.

Back at home, I'm watching my fat girl, Roxy, as I move all my things into Ross's office. She is as lost as I am without him, and I have to remind myself that the Lord is in complete control of my life. For some reason, it was Ross's time to go be with the Lord, and now this sweet dog and I have to go on alone. I must remind myself daily to trust that God knows what's best for me and will direct my steps if I choose to let him.

In times of hurting, when we don't understand the why, we must take comfort in God. Remember to ask God to hold you because He will. The hard part is that grief and healing are on His time, not ours! Still, if we trust in Him, he is always at work, and he will never fail us.

I've seen this countless times since Ross died. All of the new friends I've encountered and the resources I've found are endless. Trust me when I say that you can navigate the intricate landscape of grief through unexpected connections. So many newfound acquaintances, whether through shared experiences or chance encounters, bring fresh perspectives and understanding. These connections are vital to my healing journey, offering different vantage points and, at times, surprising sources of comfort.

As I sit here in Ross's office, which is now mine, I count all these blessings!

Purse Strings is a company led by Barb and Maggie and have endorsed this book. Found me on LinkedIn after seeing my posts about Ross. They are based out of Illinois and help women get smart about money. https://pursestrings.co/

Sean Swarner, who has endorsed this book, runs The Big Hill Challenge. It's a three-week program that helps address anxiety and PTSD. Participants spend 15 minutes a day readjusting their thinking.

Kelly Janer-Byrne, a wonderful godly woman, from the Woodbury, Chamber of Commerce, she will be the MC at the Woodbury Prayer Breakfast, at which I will be the keynote speaker. When we first met, she said a little prayer for me. She has been a cheerleader helping me get my story out and start my business.

Paul and Safaa Mercer, my neighbors and family. Not a day went by where they didn't stop over or call to check on me. God puts people in your life at different times, and he knew that at this very moment in my life I would need to live in my house and have the best neighbors a person could ever ask for.

All the Firsts
In the midst of my darkest moments, these relationships illuminated the path toward resilience and renewal, but nothing has healed me more than getting through so many of my "firsts."

It's Valentine's Day, and Ross has been gone 18 days. I'm preparing for his funeral, which is just two days away, and my house is full of people. That night, with my parents on the couch and I in the chair, the doorbell rings. At 8 p.m., I wonder who could be coming over. I open the door to find a card and cupcakes from my neighbor, Kristen. She's written the first of first are always hard, but know Ross is always with you. Of course, I burst into tears and then chuckle when I see she's signed the card from her, her boyfriend, and the dogs.

It's true we all must live life by going forward. We expect all our Valentine's Days to go as planned. But God helps us understand our life by looking back over it. I have always known that God never promises us a trouble-free life; he only promises to never leave us. And standing there on my porch on a freezing February night, I know God is with me.

Next up is spring break in March. It's the first time Noah and I have to fly off to Arizona without Ross. Every year as long as I can remember, spring break is all about being in Arizona or Florida. This "first" solemn trip is no different. We go through the motions and laugh when we can, but it's clear that nothing will ever be the same. No one says it out loud, but we all know. On our way back to the Phoenix airport, as I'm struggling to read the street signs, Noah finally calls it like it is. He says, "Mom, this is where we really need Dad. He would know exactly where to go."

And it's true, Ross always knew how to get everywhere ... even Heaven.

Our first Easter without Ross occurs one month after the funeral. I want the kids to go to church, but I end up going by myself. After church, Noah and I go over to our neighbors Paul and Saafa for brunch. When I get home, I lie in bed and cry. Noah has gone to his girlfriend's house to be with her family. I just feel so alone, and when he messages to ask if he can stay later, I lose it and text this:

"I'm by myself! I do everything for you kids, and you can't do anything for me. Stay as long as you want!"

The next thing I know, he's home and his brother Eli shows up with dinner from an amazing Italian restaurant. They place flowers on the table, and everyone apologizes to me.

Roxy is staring up at me now from her doggie bed in Ross's office. It's as if she's recalling all these firsts right alongside me.

The good ones and the bad. Like Mother's Day on May 14th when Eli and his girlfriend Taylor take me flower shopping. I think to myself this is Ross's job not mine, but the kids know that every year my Mother's Day gift was the amazing flowers Ross would plant. He would spend a few days making our front of the house and decks so beautiful, I can't help but cry thinking that now it's my job.

June 18th is our first Father's Day without Ross. Of course, I want to go to church, but the kids have other plans and don't go with me. That's okay because I'm more concerned about how the kids will cope with this day than me. I ask them how they want to honor their dad, and they suggest going to Perkins. When we arrive, memories of Eli flood in; how his tech crew would always head to Perkins for coffee and pie after shows, and how Noah followed suit when he started acting.

It's a wonderful way to remember Ross.

Following Father's Day, the day I dread the most occurs. Our first anniversary is June 22, 2023:

"Tough day today as it would have been Chico and my wedding anniversary today! He knew how much I enjoy the beach and water, so I am going to visit my long-time dearest friend and Auntie to the boys Debbie Hulbert! Looking forward for girl time, beach, the gulf, and fun time! See you soon my friend! Love you forever Ross and happy anniversary."

The next day, while still grieving, I post:

"It would have been our 14th anniversary yesterday! I can't believe it has been 5 months already since God took you to your final home in heaven! I miss you but I am so happy to know you are always looking over myself and our family! Love you forever Chico!"

The First Post-Heaven Anniversary

I fly into Fort Myers, seeking a change of scenery. Our dear friend Debbie, who couldn't make it to the funeral due to last-minute flight costs, is hosting me, and I can't wait to see her.

The ocean has always had a calming effect on me, a source of solace that I vividly remember experiencing in Mexico right after Ross passed away. So, I reached out to Debbie and asked if I could stay with her, using some spare miles I had for a plane ticket. Unfortunately, she couldn't take time off work.

My arrival on a Thursday morning is marked by an underlying stress, for it's also our anniversary. My mind races in all directions as I navigate security, and amidst this chaos, I manage to misplace my driver's license within a 25-foot radius. Panic takes hold, and TSA personnel join the frantic search. I pray fervently, pleading with God, "Where is my driver's license?" A sense of relief washes over me when I finally find it securely tucked away in the front pocket of my backpack.

Our originally scheduled 7:00 a.m. flight faces delays due to a major storm near Fort Myers. We're informed that we'll be stuck on the tarmac for two hours, with takeoff rescheduled for 9:00 a.m. Frustration mounts, but about 30 minutes later, we receive clearance for takeoff.

After reaching Debbie's place and dropping off my belongings, I head to the beach for the afternoon. The serene waters offer me a moment of peace, with few people around.

Debbie and I finally reunite after her work, and it's an emotional meeting. We haven't seen each other since Ross passed away. We both burst into tears, but it's precisely what I needed—a moment of connection.

On Friday, Debbie has to work, so I venture to Venice Beach, renowned for collecting shark teeth. It's here that I spot my first shark, its fin slicing ominously through the water, reminiscent of a scene from "Jaws."

Being alone has its perks; it allows me to reflect on Ross without distractions or obligations.

The ocean continues to be a source of healing. The resort staff in Cabo used to say, "The ocean takes your pain. It washes it away." I can attest to that. I find myself standing by the water's edge, absorbing the soothing rhythm of the waves and letting my tears flow freely.

Ross knew how much I adored the ocean and the sand. This trip feels like a tribute to him, even though he couldn't stand the humidity and would complain about the heat. I'd tease him about it, but deep down, I knew he'd have booked a trip here.

I've been immersing myself in books, following daily devotions, and praying consistently. It's been instrumental in my healing journey. I understand that the pain will never fully vanish, but each day has indeed become more manageable, just as the books suggest. Initially, it feels overwhelming, with thoughts like, "How will I manage everything—the house, bills, and parenting Noah?" Returning to work immediately after Ross passed keeps me occupied, but when I have moments of solitude, grief sneaks in, particularly at night. Being alone offers moments of introspection—a chance to think about Ross and navigate the process of healing.

One thing's for sure, I want to live my life as a shining light for God! As non-believers watch me, I want them to see me responding to this horrific tragedy with grace. If I can help one person come to know God and start a personal relationship with him then I am doing the work that God has asked of me.

And I know He will comfort me through my friends, family, new connections and of course, even Ross.

It's August now, nearly seven months since I lost the love of my life, and needless to say, it hasn't been easy trying to find my way in my new life. Trying to figure out who I am as Candy Wolff the widow has been impossible. Yet today, out of nowhere, I see a text message pop up on my phone from Ross! I still have him in my contacts as my #1 favorite, and it's showing a text from him that reads, "Call me!"

My heart drops as I wonder to myself, "How in the heck did whoever has his phone number get connected to me?!" Seconds later, when I go into my message app to respond, the text message is gone. I truly believe it was a reminder from God that Ross is still with me. I feel so lucky to be aware of all the little signs that I see reminding me how he is my guardian angel!

If you have lost a loved one, be aware of all the little things they try to show you. It's amazing how much it will mean to you.

A favorite reminder for me is how Google Photos presents daily memories of all the fun adventures we had together and with family and friends.

Chapter 6

Love's Last Dance

You don't know what I am doing now, but
you will understand later.
~John 13:7

For the last 12 hours, I wasn't sure if we were going to go to Cabo or not. There is a hurricane coming toward Cabo, which is ironic because that's how I would describe my feelings right now. I'm a big hurricane of not knowing what to expect. My anxiety is high as this is going to be a tough one. I am blessed to have my dear friend and neighbor, Safaa, taking me to the airport, as she has been a complete rock star for me over the last nine months.

Yesterday, before making the decision to go to Cabo or not, I reached out to my guardian angel, Ahtziri, to let her know I am coming and asked her about the possible hurricane because it just adds another layer of anxiety to everything. There was a big hurricane around 2015 or 2016 that destroyed Cabo, even the airport! So, I know God's going to take care of me, and it will be fine. Ahtziri told me not to worry about anything and that I should come to Cabo. Once again, she calmed my nerves if only for a night.

So, my flight is at 6:00 a.m. this morning. I'll get into Phoenix and then have a layover and then head to Cabo and should get in at about 12:30 p.m., and Vass will be there waiting for me. The word I'd use is tumultuous. Lots of different feelings right now. I'm anxious about leaving the kids even though I know they'll be fine. Anxious about going back to the last place Ross and I were together.

I make it through the security check. Having only gotten a few hours of sleep last night, I am one exhausted, anxious person. Ross's ashes are in my suitcase. I didn't want to worry about them being in my carry-on. We'll start boarding the plane soon. Thank God my psychiatrist prescribed that Xanax, otherwise I'd be a complete mess. I'm not a great flier as it is, and then knowing that I'm going back down to Cabo is almost too much. No tears yet, but I would imagine once I get on the plane … actually, my eyes are starting to tear up right now as I think about being back there. So, yeah, this is going to be tough.

Siting on the plane waiting for everyone else to board, I feel a wave of weakness wash over me. I see my phone lighting up and catch a glimpse of the text from my brother-in-law Reed. He's letting me know I can reach out if I need anything. That gives me some comfort I was looking for.

I fall dead asleep as soon as we're airborne. And then of course, my favorite thing—I think Ross maybe is doing this to tease me—horrible turbulence. So, I wake up and can't get back to sleep. It's worth it though. Bursting in, over the back wing, is the most beautiful sunrise I've ever seen.

After landing safely at the Phoenix International Airport, my anxiety sneaks back in. It looks like the tropical storm is turning into a hurricane and will hit Cabo on Saturday. I say a little prayer under my breath, asking God to redirect it. Of course, I wouldn't mind a thunderstorm, but oh Lord, to have two terrible trips to Cabo, that would be a lot. I shake off these dark thoughts and remind myself that God is good, it's going to be great, and everything is all right for now.

When I finally arrive in Cabo, I breathe a sigh of relief. I have no trouble getting through customs, which is my biggest fear after all the issues with the police after Ross's death. The *last* thing I want is to end up back at the police station wondering if I will ever make it home.

It's weird being here in Cabo without Ross. His absence is palpable, especially in a place we used to love together. I miss him a lot. Vass, my loyal companion, keeps me busy with a long walk and pool time, helping me navigate mixed emotions.

Tonight is a bit challenging, especially with Ross's ashes beside me. On top of everything, there's the added stress of an approaching hurricane. I talk to Noah, who, despite being my son, has taken on the role of looking out for me, checking to see if we have a plan for the impending storm.

The next few days are expected to be unpleasant with rain, limiting my outdoor activities. Nevertheless, I'm grateful we get to take walks and be outside as much as possible. Sitting on the patio, watching the waves come in, I know the storm will be huge. It's coming, and there's nothing we can do to prevent it.

Vass and I head out for a quick walk. We pass the shops that Ross and I used to frequent, but I'm too emotional to go inside. I still haven't made it down to the ocean yet; maybe tomorrow morning before the storm hits. The yearning for Ross is tough. The support from friends has been incredible. My mother-in-law, Rich, and Eli, call me to check in as well. All the while I can't stop thinking about how cute Noah is. He's just so worried, but I assure him that we have a plan and that everything is fine. I'm encouraged by his attention because he really didn't want anything to do with coming down here. Despite this, he still asks me what good food I've eaten and if I got any guacamole because he knows this is something that Ross and I always talked about—the amazing guacamole and chips.

When I talked to Noah, I mentioned that we all needed to come down and he agrees. So hopefully maybe in the next year. It would be cool to come down with all the kids and even have the kids spread more of Ross's ashes with me. This trip, I only brought a little baggy since I had no idea what was going to happen. And I didn't want to take any chances because I was scared to death to go through customs with any of his ashes, let alone all of them.

At the end of the night, sheer exhaustion hits me, and I crash.

When I wake up, I indulge in some pool time, basking in the sound of the waves. I repeatedly tell Vass that his place is truly heaven on earth. It's surreal to think that this haven is where I lost Ross.

As the hurricane starts moving, I start to think I should scatter some of his ashes outside the front of Vass's house in the flower garden. Then, on Tuesday, his birthday, weather permitting, I'll complete the ritual by the ocean. My days are filled with joy, but the nights are lonelier than I ever thought possible.

On my second day in Cabo, the hurricane is making its presence felt. I manage to spend a bit of time in the hot tub, which overlooks the Sea of Cortez. The rain is light, almost serene, a calm before the storm as they say. I sit there, watching the waves, and can't help but be reminded of Ross. Our shared love for the water and the sound of waves crashing on the shore is something special. Today, the waves are massive.

Amidst some work, we venture out to a nearby pizza place in the sprinkling rain and have one of the best wood-stone pizzas I've ever tasted. Vass and I attempt to walk down to the beach, but the impending hurricane causing sea swelling means we can't reach it.

My thoughts are consumed with the hope that by Tuesday, despite the hurricane, I'll be able to walk down to the beach and scatter the rest of Ross's ashes in the ocean. My mind seems to be more on the hurricane than anything else. I find solace in texting a friend, playfully calling it "Hurricane Chico" after Ross, who was indeed a force of nature. I miss and love him deeply.

Interestingly, my room overlooks the Sea of Cortez in a large horseshoe shape, providing a view of numerous lights in the distance. I can't help but wonder what others are thinking in this moment. The previous couple of days, workers had secured the palm trees against the wind, and people had been reinstalling hurricane shutters that had been taken down, as hurricanes typically occur from August to September, and it is now October. The whole situation is quite surreal.

Currently, the hurricane is making its way upon shore. It is a category 2 with lots of rain and very heavy winds. 't's expected to drop over 10 inches of rain, with the tail end winds of the hurricane winds to reach over 70 miles per hour. The situation is intense: it's dark, visibility is minimal, and the wind is audibly roaring. Fortunately, I've been assured my current location of my room is secure.

I've never been in a hurricane before so am asking the Lord, "Am I not supposed to be here? Was I not supposed to come back down to Mexico?" So many different thoughts are going through my head. But I really do want to spread his ashes on Tuesday, October 24th, as it would have been his 56th birthday in remembrance of him and set my heart free to be able to move forward.

Maybe God's sending the storm to help me keep my mind off that. And remind me of how he is in control of everything. It's just like the name of this book, "Lost and Found in Mexico."

It seems like I do find myself closer to God when I'm down here because I am. I just rely on Him so much more down here than I do when I'm at home. And He is so good to me. So, maybe I ended up in this country during a hurricane, so I'll never forget who God is and what He means to me.

God is good. And I'm going to get through this. I'm in a safe room. I can put up with this for a couple more days and then Tuesday, hopefully it will be beautiful and I can get down to the ocean to set Ross free and maybe enjoy a little more sun before I go home.

As night falls, fear takes hold of us again. It's crazy how during the day you can handle the hurricane at a different level of stress than when night falls. The sound of shattering glass proves to be a ceramic light fixture just outside my window. I find it challenging to fully process these events, but I hold onto the hope that future trips with my boys will be filled with sunshine, safety, and no hurricanes.

I managed to sleep off and on, waking up intermittently to the intense winds. The doors, especially to my room, kept banging due to the force of the winds. The sea is tumultuous, reflecting the anger of the storm.

It's the morning of October 21st, and last night felt like one of the longest I've ever had. Hurricane Norma brought 80-mile-per-hour winds, and the rain was absolutely relentless. The house is soaked, with water seeping in everywhere, palm tree branches strewn about, and some tiles lifted off the roof. The power of God, showcased in the relentless pounding of the wind against the windows, is awe-inspiring.

As of now, it looks like the hurricane is taking a turn to go north, which is a relief. However, there's always the concern it could change direction and come back at us. The winds were projected to reach 100 mph today, but currently, they're sustained at around 50-60 mph, with gusts up to 80 mph in the morning. The house is a mess, and at the moment, it's windy without rain, requiring a squeegee to remove the inches of water on the tile floors.

I'm staying in touch with my mother-in-law, my kids, my parents, and friends, assuring them that I'm safe. It's quite an experience, marking the second time I've faced such a storm in Cabo.

On Sunday morning, I find a huge mess in the wake of the hurricane. We are finally able to go outside today, and I spend hours trying to find drains and clean them off so water can drain off the upper patios and then down by the pool.

There are at least six inches of standing water that I have to wade through and a lot of debris. The drains are clogged from all the debris, so it's another clean-up day, but at least it's cleaning up outside the house now. And today it is almost a blessing in disguise because I have been so busy dealing with this, I haven't had time to be anxious or sad.

I text with Ahtziri and unfortunately, because of the hurricane, I won't be able to see her or any of the guys at the resort. She feels bad because she told me it was safe to come down, and now the hurricane has hit, but I tell her it's not her fault. No one can predict the weather.

We're all safe. God protected us. So, it's good. My mission was to come down here to spread ashes—and that's what I'm going to do on Ross's birthday, which is in one day.

I'm able to get a little pool time, for maybe an hour. This hurricane is unbelievable and it's just a category two. It's nothing compared to some of the storms others have been through. Still, it's scary. The crashing waves last night reminded me that this is yet another experience I can no longer share with Ross.

However, this trip I don't have a car, so I'm kind of stuck at the house. It's wonderful to be here, but I miss going downtown Cabo and seeing what's new. That was something that Ross and I enjoyed doing. So, I miss it. I didn't realize how much I would miss it, but I do. And it's kind of lonely, even though I am here with a friend. I am lonely.

On Tuesday, when I spread Ross's ashes, I am hoping to honor him. But I want to be able to move forward. Because I know he's not coming back. He's always going to be a part of me and our family, and it's been lonely at home, but it's another thing being lonely in a foreign country.

It's funny because I never felt this lonely when Ross passed. Because I had everybody at the resort and, granted, I have a very dear friend here keeping me busy and making me laugh and I love him to death. He's amazing, but it's different. I don't even know how to explain the difference, but I'm hoping to find that peace again on Tuesday when I go to spread Ross's ashes.

Still, there's no time for that now. I have to clean up more inside the house and outside the house. Vass keeps telling me I'm such a hard worker. And it just makes me laugh because Ross was a hard worker. We had that in common. When something needed to be done, we just did it. And that's who I am, even more so now that Ross is gone. Whenever I see an issue or a mess or something that needs fixing, I'm the one that has to do it now.

It's strange how other people look at you and make comments that you just don't see. I've always been a doer. I look at the mess and I think, "All right, what would Ross do? What would be his solution to fix this?" Because he would always have one. And so, I feel like over the last couple of days he's been in my head telling me what I need to do and how to fix everything.

The pool, too, needs attention, revealing a substantial amount of dirt and debris, including large palm tree fragments. Despite the challenges, the process of clearing and salvaging offers a distraction and a semblance of control over the chaos.

As I reflect, I realize the importance of work in keeping my mind occupied. Support from friends and acquaintances checking in on me during the hurricane has been invaluable. The care and concern extended by both local and distant friends have been a source of strength.

In a few days, on October 27th, it will be nine months since he left us. Since then, I've undergone substantial personal growth. I've become stronger, more independent, and bolder. The fear that once held me back has diminished, allowing me to approach life with a newfound courage. The perspective on what matters and the importance of expressing oneself has shifted, acknowledging the unpredictable nature of life.

It's indeed remarkable to observe the transformation and adaptation that has occurred. As I prepare to honor Ross's memory, I carry with me the strength and wisdom gained from the journey of the past nine months.

This is more than just a reflection on celebrating Ross and his profound significance in my life. It's also a celebration of the person I've become over the last nine months, rediscovering myself in the process. The initial months after Ross's passing were a blur, with the funeral and a few scattered memories, but it was during spring break in Arizona that I began to truly comprehend the journey ahead.

I got through the early months with a relentless cycle of work, tending to Noah and his volleyball, and staying occupied with household tasks. I intentionally avoided slowing down to process the weight of the situation. Evenings were the only time reality would set in, and I'd find solace in tears before drifting off to sleep.

Now, as we walk by the ocean for the first time since the hurricane last Wednesday, memories flood back. It is a reminder of our shared love for adventure, climbing rocks, and pushing boundaries.

Sitting by the water, I feel a connection, an unspoken tie to Ross. There is an inexplicable desire to stay in the water, and although it might sound irrational, it feels right. I collect numerous pieces of coral and shells, imagining Ross laughing at my growing collection. Coral, especially, takes on a new significance, symbolizing beauty, rarity, and, in this instance, a precious gift from him.

Chapter 7

Until We Meet Again

Yet you do not know what tomorrow will bring.
What is your life? For you are a mist that
appears for a little time and then vanishes.
~James 4:14

Today is October 24th, and it's Ross's birthday. He would have been his 56th, and I'm on my way to the Sea of Cortez to spread his ashes. It is overwhelming and crazy because I feel like he is with me. Still, I know that he's not. And this *first* is the worst yet. He should be here celebrating his birthday with me, not watching me from Heaven carry his ashes into the ocean.

Still, I press on. I'm convinced this final goodbye is going to mean something big. If I can succeed and just get this over with, I will find peace. He will be released from my heart, and I can move on. I want to be able to bring the boys to Mexico and show them all the places we visited together. That will never happen under the weight of this much grief. I've got to let him go.

As I step into the water, a huge wave hits and nearly knocks me on my butt. I laugh hysterically, thinking, "Oh my gosh, Ross would have loved this huge wave!"

Maybe he's giving me a hug? Perhaps he's letting me know he's here with me? And with that, peace washes over me. My heart is still, and I feel an abundance of love. It's the exact same feeling I had the day I held his lifeless body in my arms. It's the perfect mix of wanting to go home so badly and also feeling like I'm leaving him here all over again, which hurts.

I think of Proverbs 3:5-6, *Trust in the Lord with all your heart do not depend on your own understanding. Seek his will in all you do, and he will show you which path to take.*

I believe I am doing God's will by letting Ross go, and with that, I scatter his ashes into the sea. The water is calm minus a few waves, so different from the power that crashed through during the hurricane. The sun is shining. It's absolutely beautiful, and Ross would have loved it. It's a perfect 82 degrees, and the humidity is gone. What a wonderful birthday this would have been for him. I can almost hear him praising the weather and applauding the day.

On my walk back, I collect more corals and seashells that were stirred up by Hurricane Norma. This is something that I love to do, and I have vases full of seashells at home. The hurricane has blessed me with so much coral, and I can't wait to make a little vase of all my coral that I can put next to Ross's urn and picture for him. I can absolutely hear him laughing at me for scooping up even more seashells, saying, "When will you have enough?!" I reply into the wind, "Never."

Once I reach Vass's, I settle into a little work. I have a call with my coworker, and he tells me I should probably stay far away from Mexico forever. I say, "You know what? I lost my husband down here. I made it through a hurricane. What else could happen?"

The truth is all who listen to God will live in peace untroubled by fear of harm (Proverbs 1:33). Besides, I could never stay away from Cabo. Today proved once again that Ross is here with me. I feel closer to him in Cabo than anywhere else.

Which my heart breaks knowing that I'm leaving Cabo tomorrow. But I'm so glad I did this. Before bed, I talk with the boys, and everything is good with them. My poor mother-in-law though had a rough day. And Ross's best friend Rich, bless his heart, I learn that he had a cigar in honor of Ross, something they always did on Ross's birthday.

I miss my kids and my dog, but I have this brokenness. The loneliness that I felt when I left Cabo before is lingering. It's not a good feeling, and I hope someday when I come back, I'll be free from it. I want to bring the boys here and not be plagued by this never-ending sense that I'm abandoning my husband. I need to believe there is hope that I can get over this feeling that I'm leaving him behind. Even though I know he's in a better place, it's still hard.

I pack everything up and prepare for the long day of travel. I'll get home at midnight tomorrow night, but I'm so glad I made it through today. I accomplished what I set out to do. Unfortunately, I wasn't able to see my friends from the resort, but I was able to at least text with them.

Today I am flying home from Cabo now. It's hard to leave. It reminds me of my return trip on Delta after Ross died. It takes my breath away when I walk through the airport doors. The first thing I see, in my mind's eye, is the Delta agent, and all of those emotions begin flooding my body as I recall how he must have thought I was crazy. It's an out-of-body experience like no other. I remember how gracious they were to me when they learned I had my husband's ashes. And how management jumped in and didn't charge me for the overage on my bags and moved me up to have a better seat on the plane. They took such great care of me.

Moving through the airport now, feeling grateful, I try to find that first agent who helped me or the manager who met me at the counter, but I don't see anyone and, honestly, I start thinking, "Would I even know them if I saw them?" I can't even recall what they looked like because I was in such a daze trying to get home to my boys.

Back then, I was so angry with the police for everything they did to me. I felt violated by them for stealing all my money and personal belongings when they did their investigation right after Ross died. This time around, after being in Cabo for a week and being isolated with the hurricane, not getting out for three days, I have no anger. This is a relief to me. It means I'm getting better. I'm healing and that anger I thought might be tucked away is nearly gone.

I have peace and make it into Phoenix with no issues, but then of course, I encounter delays. So, I have time to think. I realize I flew down to Cabo by myself to scatter Ross's ashes in the Sea of Cortez and to be with God. It was just me and God when Ross passed, and it was just me and God when I said my final goodbye.

And now I know that I can go back. I'm even excited for my next trip. I can't wait to be in Cabo with my boys or with my friends. Next time, I'll go to the shops and all our favorite places. I'll sit by the ocean and listen to the waves and walk the beaches and be 100% fine.

I finally arrive home at 1:30 a.m. on October 26th after traveling for 19 hours. Tomorrow it will be nine months since Ross has passed. And I, honestly, in the last nine months, never ever thought that I could find happiness. And I do miss him every day, but the fact that I can look forward to bringing the boys, which is something I never thought I would be able to do, gives me hope.

All these, *firsts* truly suck. Everyone is right about that. And I still have three more months of *firsts* to get through. I knew the fall would be hard because of Ross's birthday and college football, which he loved. Hunting season is coming up, and he used to always go to Edgerton for five days to spend time with his cousins, deer and pheasant hunting. And then there's Thanksgiving, another holiday that Ross loved. We always watched football, and he'd make fun of me because I had the parade on while I was starting the turkey.

Getting back from Mexico and knowing what I have in front of me the next three months is hard. Ross absolutely loved Christmas. He loved watching the boys open their presents because he loved to give people gifts. He was such a giver. So, of course, Christmas is going to be tough, and then there's New Year's, my birthday, Noah's birthday, and then January 27th will mark Ross's one-year heavenly birthday. But I know I have a new outlook after being in Cabo. I know I can handle anything.

Hurricanes are bad, but God brought good for me out of this one. It helped me get through some hard days, giving me work to do to keep my mind off my pain. All I can say is God is good. He was with me the whole time. I felt him with me, and I felt such warmth on the plane coming home from Cabo.

So, all in all, one of the hardest—but also rewarding—trips I ever took. It is helping me heal so I can move on, and God knew that's what I needed.

Ross is always going to be a part of my life. He's always going to be there, and I can move forward, and I can still love him, and I know that God loves me so much. There is a reason why he took Ross, and whatever happens, he'll bring good out of it. I truly believe I can see my future and how I'm going to be able to help people because of the loss I had nine months ago.

The holidays are generally good, although Christmas Eve brings some challenges. My mother-in-law, brother-in-law, and my mother-in-law's sister join us, and despite some tears and hugs, we manage to get through it. Christmas morning feels strange with just Noah and me, but we later gather with the in-laws, and once again, tears are shed as we navigate the day.

New Year's Eve passes without much event, but my 51st birthday on January 7th hits me unexpectedly hard. I have been doing well, so the sudden wave of emotions overwhelms me. Waking up that morning, I find myself crying uncontrollably, reminiscent of the difficult days almost a year ago when I discovered Ross's death.

Noah, my son, sweetly decorates for my birthday, trying to make the day special. However, it's the absence of the customary birthday card and pink roses from Ross that weighs heavily on me. I spend the day crying, finding solace in conversations with my mother-in-law and parents.

Noah, understanding the significance, prepares dinner, and Eli and Taylor bring a birthday cake, attempting to make the day as special as possible. Despite their efforts, the absence of Ross's gestures makes for a tough day. I'm mad that I'm grieving so much, thinking I was through the worst of it, and now my birthday sneaks up like a foreign attack. I barely make it through the day, and the pain never leaves.

On January 9th, Noah turns 18, and we celebrate at the casino, trying to keep the day positive. We make it through all the firsts without Ross—first holidays, first birthdays, each bringing its own set of challenges.

As I approach the one-year mark since Ross's passing on January 27th, I find myself reflecting on our shared memories. Each day, I recall moments from our time together, including the last days in Mexico before everything changed on that fateful Friday morning at 7:11 a.m., January 27th, 2023.

Chapter 8

Empowering Others

Hug your loved ones and let them know you love them every chance you get as you never know when that last chance will happen!
~Candy Wolff

When your life turns upside down from the death of a loved one, your brain protects you by shutting down. It can seem like you are walking around in a fog. Your mind plays tricks on you, and clear thoughts are a thing of the past. You can barely remember your own name, let alone someone else's. Everything becomes about getting to the next second, the next turn around the ever-winding corners of your once straight and narrow life.

As the sole provider for my son, getting my finances in order is my top priority. And boy, have I learned a lot since the fateful day when I arrived home from the horrific ordeal in Cabo, without the love of my life, and had no choice but to accept reality. Ross, who hadn't worked full time for several years, had been dipping into the 401(k) to subsidize our income. He hadn't kept it a secret from me, but the extent of the money that was gone was a secret. I knew it was happening, could sense the stress he felt because of it, but what I didn't know, that I now know all too well, is that the account was completely empty.

All that was left was a check for 60,000 dollars. I had no other money to my name, a celebration of life to pay for, and a zero balance in our retirement account. The fogginess surrounding my brain made it nearly impossible to comprehend the dire straits I was truly in. I discovered the most devastating financial situation I could have ever imagined in the midst of the greatest grief of my life. The horrors were right in front of me, but all I could see were the tears welling up in my eyes.

It didn't take long to realize I had no clue about our bills, and the thought that Noah and I could lose the house hit me like a ton of bricks. How did I get to a place where that could even happen? I thought I was responsible and prepared for anything. The truth is I was reckless. I let someone else take the full reins of my financial security, and now he was gone. And with him, he took my security. So, the promise I made to Noah that first night to stay in our home became a vow of redemption, and it still holds true today. I have become a financial steward. I am now clear on my bills and what I need to make in order to keep my home and have enough for retirement.

If anything like this happens to you, you must be ready.

STEP 1:

Notify your bank to stop all automatic payments. You never know. There could be payments that you are not required to pay.

STEP 2:

Identify top priority bills—mortgage and utilities—and pay them manually. This means you have to know who your mortgage, water, heat, cable, phone, and electricity providers are.

Yes, automatic payments and e-billing have made our lives easier, but not when you're dealing with the death of a spouse. In that case, all you want is your mailman to bring you a paper bill, so you know your account numbers, how much you have to pay, and when you have to pay.

The one thing everyone told me, over and over, right after Ross died, is, "You must make your mortgage payment." I wanted to scream, "I agree, but I don't know who my mortgage lender is, so how can I pay THEM?!"

This book is my gift to you, my readers. If I can help even one person avoid the pitfalls I have endured, it will all be worth it. I never want anyone to be hit with the issues that blackened both my eyes. The bruise to my right eye was grief and to my left eye was money. Trust me, neither can be ignored.

I highly recommend you have a money conversation with your significant other today. It's not easy or fun, but it is necessary. For help, go to https://pursestrings.co/ and download free worksheets authored by Dr. Barb Provost and Maggie Nielsen, MBA. Purse Strings also provides financial professionals who will work alongside you to make financial decisions. There is nothing more important than knowing your loved ones will be able to grieve without having all the financial woes that I had.

Give your family the best gift you could ever give them and don't keep secrets about finances. TALK, TALK, TALK before it's too late!

Here is the list of items that I had to deal with from the moment I got home from Cabo. Despite needing to plan a celebration of life and be strong for my boys, everything was made 1000 times worse by such unnecessary financial struggles. Please make sure you have the answers to the following items:

- Who is your financial advisor?
- Make sure all your bank accounts are joint accounts.
- Know where all the paperwork for all our insurance policies (life, house, car, home, umbrella)

- Know who your mortgage company is and what your payment is.
- Know which credit cards you both have.
- Learn the passcodes to your safety deposit boxes.
- Learn the passcodes to your physical safes.
- Learn cell phone password.
- Learn computer password.
- Learn email passwords.
- Learn social media account passwords.
- Learn the Wi-Fi passcodes.
- Making sure both names are on the mortgage, all vehicles, investments, life insurance, utilities (water, gas, heat, garbage, electric, cable, internet)

We believed we'd rebuild our savings. But in the end, it became a significant issue. Even if someone prefers not to know, they must be aware. Knowing where crucial documents are kept and the source of your income is essential. Also, both partners must have access to important accounts, like at the bank. Otherwise, you might find yourself in a tough situation.

Understanding the ins and outs of your monthly expenses and tracking where your money is going all come down to having conversations and demolishing traditional walls that were designed to shield someone from financial stress. In the end, being upfront and transparent about your financial situation is the key to financial stability and peace of mind.

To be better prepared for these situations, I realized the importance of keeping records of passcodes for phones, computers, and email accounts. Ensure that all accounts have specified beneficiaries to avoid complications.

We have three safes at home, and I know all the codes and have the keys to access them. Thankfully, my son remembered the code for one safe and the keys for gun cases. A fingerprint recognition doesn't work after a person's death, so know the alternative method to access it. As for Ross's phone, even though my name was on the account, it required a court order to access because it was locked with his password. It was a battle I didn't want to pursue, as you will find out what you have energy for and what you don't. It's ok to be honest with yourself about what you can handle and what you can't.

One last thing I would love to leave you with: have a conversation about funeral arrangements as well as burial or cremation. It will make everything much easier. When you can't think because of a mental fog, it's hard to know what your loved one would want you to do. Also, please take care of yourself! You don't want to find out your loved one was hiding something from you because if you learn the truth after they're gone, there's no way to have a conversation. You'll be left, like I was, with nothing more than a journal to help you take steps toward forgiveness and love despite what may be perceived as betrayal.

Don't let a day go by that you don't tell your loved ones they mean the world to you and that you love them! I never told Ross I loved him before he died, and that is one thing I will live with the rest of my life while on earth until my Lord and Savior brings me to my final resting place in Heaven!

Epilogue

Guard your heart above all else, for it
determines the course of your life.
~Proverbs 4:23

As I look back over the last year of my life and all the things I have learned, I am proud to say, with God by my side I have become a stronger woman than I ever thought would be possible, I have grown spiritually closer to God in the last year, and he has shown me that even when I don't think I have the strength to take the next breath or step, he is with me. With him I can do anything!

I have learned to journal my thoughts, as it's hard for people to understand what I am going through unless they have lost a spouse themselves. I have read many books on being a widow, grieving and even on heaven. I have accomplished Sean Swaner's The Big Hill Challenge, which I would recommend for anyone dealing with PTSD, anxiety, and depression. I was blessed to meet Dr. Barb Provost from Purse String and had the opportunity to share my story with her and her daughter Maggie Nelson on the Purse Strings Podcast. I am looking forward to my first keynote speech to tell my story and hopefully help one more person. For some reason, God has blessed me with a story to tell, and I am fully committed to the purpose he has trusted me with and will continue to help people in any way I can!

I have been blessed to meet so many wonderful people who have helped me along my journey, and can't thank all my friends and family enough for the support they have provide for myself and the boys.

As for where my life is heading next…only God knows, but what I do know is I don't take one second of this life for granted anymore. I will love with all my heart and make sure all my loved ones know every day that I love them so that when it's my time to join Ross, there is no doubt what they mean to me.

I am ready to begin the next chapter of my life, living it to the fullest every day with God first and leading the way with my faith! The boys and I are ready for our next adventure!

References

Purse Strings
Owners: Dr. Barb Provost and Maggie Nielsen, MBA
https://pursestrings.co

Sean Swarner
The Big Hill Challenge
https://www.seanswarner.com

Books:
The Hot Young Widows Club
By Nora McInerny

Imagine Heaven
By John Burke

Grief One Day at a Time
By Alan D Wolfelt, PH.D

Final Words

Discover a riveting journey of resilience and self-discovery in Candy Wolff's compelling book, "Lost and Found in Mexico: A Widow's Road to Recovery." This is a must-read for every woman! Wolff lays bare her vulnerable and authentic life story, navigating the tumultuous highs and lows that resonate with many of us. From the complexities of marriage and divorce to the challenges of raising children and facing the daily struggles of life, Candy invites us into her personal world, allowing us to experience the full spectrum of emotions.

In this captivating narrative, we share in Candy's stress, concerns, worries, and the fluttering excitement of newfound love. Her story becomes a mirror reflecting our own experiences, and we can't help but nod and think, "Yep, been there!"

However, Candy's journey takes an unexpected turn, revealing a sadly common yet shocking reality. Through

her words, she imparts valuable lessons for women everywhere. This book is a poignant reminder of the importance of understanding and actively managing finances within the household, dispelling assumptions that things are taken care of.

While Candy's story is heart-wrenching, it echoes the stories of many, and it's this awareness that prompted the creation of Purse Strings. "Lost and Found in Mexico" not only captures the personal struggles of one woman but also serves as a beacon for others, encouraging financial empowerment and resilience. Don't miss out on this inspiring narrative that goes beyond personal pain to advocate for change and awareness.

~**Barbara J. Provost, EdD**
Founder, Purse Strings, LLC